The Power and Form of

Emerson's Thought

The Power and Form
of Emerson's Thought

Jeffrey L. Duncan

University Press of Virginia

Charlottesville

THE UNIVERSITY PRESS OF VIRGINIA
Copyright © 1973 by the Rector and Visitors
of the University of Virginia

First published 1973

ISBN: 0-8139-0510-9
Library of Congress Catalog Card Number: 73-85043
Printed in the United States of America

To Floyd Stovall

Contents

The mind is urged to ask for one cause of many effects; then for the cause of that; and again the cause, diving still into the profound: self-assured that it shall arrive at an absolute and sufficient one—a one that shall be all. "In the midst of the sun is the light, in the midst of the light is truth, and in the midst of truth is the imperishable being," say the Vedas. All philosophy, of East and West, has the same centripetence. Urged by an opposite necessity, the mind returns from the one to that which is not one, but other or many; from cause to effect; and affirms the necessary existence of variety, the self-existence of both, as each is involved in the other. These strictly-blended elements it is the problem of thought to separate and to reconcile. Their existence is mutually contradictory and exclusive; and each so fast slides into the other that we can never say what is one, and what it is not. The Proteus is as nimble in the highest as in the lowest grounds; when we contemplate the one, the true, the good—as in the surfaces and extremities of matter.

"Plato"

Life itself is a mixture of power and form, and will not bear the least excess of either. To finish the moment, to find the journey's end in every step of the road, to live the greatest number of good hours, is wisdom.

"Experience"

Human life is made up of the two elements, power and form, and the proportion must be invariably kept if we would have it sweet and sound.

"Experience"

Preface

IF NOTHING ELSE, Emerson is a cerebral writer. (Too cerebral, many feel.) Ideas are his central concern, and it is precisely his ideas that get in the way of many twentieth-century readers. We have fallen out of sympathy with the notions of a moral order in nature, an innate moral sense in man, self-reliance, compensation, the essential negation of evil, an aggressive optimism: they do not tally with our experience. And Emerson never puts his ideas into a rationally comprehensible order. Not only does he change his mind from time to time, he contradicts himself, from essay to essay, paragraph to paragraph, sentence to sentence. We have to read him, finally, with grave reservations, even impatient disbelief.

Yet we have to read him—the man can write: if only sentences here and there, they are brilliant sentences, rich and taut. And if a man can write, we feel he must have something to say. So we look for those ideas that have remained credible: his organicism, for instance, his concept of symbol, his emphasis on perception. But we have also discovered his preoccupation with the very process of thought, discovered how subtly he can depict the life of an idea. This is the essential Emerson, we surmise, a man thinking, and we begin to turn toward his journals, the better to observe him in the act. Thus we can salvage him.

But we also distort him, and perhaps certain principles as well. We focus on his thinking and forget the thought, as if the two have only an incidental relation. We assume that thinking is good, whereas in and of itself, no matter how keen, it is just another activity. The value of an idea depends on the thinking, the manner in which it is developed, to be sure, but so must the value of thinking depend on its idea. In either case, the thought is indispensable. To believe otherwise courts decadence. We cannot admire Emerson's thinking, it seems to me, without respecting his ideas. We should, therefore, prefer their finished statement in the essays—Emerson's art—to their formulation in rough draft—the journals. And we cannot choose to respect only those ideas we find readily compatible (an assertion, admittedly, which Emerson himself would be the first to deny). His ideas, both the foolish and the sensible, are integral. His concept of symbolism, for example, derives from his quasi idealism; so does his theory of perception, and his notion of a moral order. We may find certain ideas out of context useful, but to understand Emerson's use of them —to appreciate his art—we cannot ignore the context. And if we find certain of his ideas agreeable, we should find the others respectable.

We have not, despite the fine criticism Emerson has amply received. We have had difficulty seeing his ideas through our own assumptions—the assumptions, that is, of American middle-class liberal academic intellectuals (those vague words we know the meaning of). And the recent reaction against those assumptions may have given our relationship with Emerson difficulty, too. Formerly we tended to hold with the later, more conservative Emerson; now the earlier, headier one is more the vogue. Either preference presumes that we can pick and choose, and that, after the example of Whicher, there are Emersons to pick and choose among.

This essay tends to deny the convenience of such a choice. To parcel out Emerson involves, I believe, certain misapprehensions. Let us take his concept of freedom as a crucial example: the adjectives *perfect, complete, absolute,* and the like crop up in discussions of the earlier egoistical Emerson's notion of freedom (as opposed to his later resignation to fate, indomitable or sad), but those adjectives imply a philosophical naiveté we cannot ascribe to him. If one were absolutely free, one could do anything one wished with impunity, such as stepping off a cliff. This would be particularly true of Emerson's concept in that he believed in the close correspondence of the spiritual and physical worlds. That such an instance is absurd is my point. But then, it can be asserted, Emerson does invite the reader, at the end of *Nature,* to build his own world, and when he does such things as snakes, spiders, and prisons, indeed all "disagreeable appearances," will vanish. I find it compatible with the peroration of "Fate": with a revolution of spirit we will see the "beautiful necessity" of such things—in the case of prisons and such, a moral order working itself out—the appearances will no longer be disagreeable, i.e., they will no longer be regarded as manifestations of an essential evil. In both essays it is the way we see, not what we see, that matters. There our freedom lies. (Morally, I would like to add, absolute freedom is Iago's ruling assumption—a position Emerson consistently rejected with all his strength.)

Then why does he make the same point so differently? The issue requires exploration from the other side, so to speak, and I do not wish to deny that Emerson shifted emphasis to that other side. Nevertheless I believe that the shift in emphasis has been transformed into an irreconcilable about-face. I believe that I have discovered an underlying coherence in Emerson's thought. I say *discovered* because I did not seek it to support a hunch. Yet, for the sake of economy, the form of my essay presumes that coherence. It means, though, taking statements disparate in time and putting them side by side. I have tried to pay scrupulous attention to the context of each and to make only those juxtapositions that are valid in the hope that the reader can see the compatibility. Where there is a difference, I acknowledge it. The form I have chosen implies that I take Emerson's ideas literally, that I take him at face value. Now current in Emerson criticism is the word *strategy*: it implies that Emerson says one thing when he really means another, or puts forward one idea in order to thrust home another before the reader is aware of it. I disagree with this notion. I find Emerson tough and subtle enough at face value—marvelously tough, wondrously subtle. And while I do not regard him as a philosopher, I believe it is necessary to understand his ideas, their structure and relation, to appreciate his art. It is in that belief that I submit the following essay.

The subject of the essay is the power and form of Emerson's thought, i.e., his concept of polarity. I could have used other terms—the "unity and variety," the "spirit and body"—but "power and form" (the terms Emerson uses in the essay "Experience") seem to me the most inclusive and suggestive. After describing and analyzing the significance of polarity in his examinations of nature, society, and the individual, in that order, I attempt a reappraisal of his optimism, not as a last word—Emerson is too large and varied for last words—but as another beginning, a keener sympathy with an astonishingly keen artist.

To avoid innumerable notes I shall cite my two major sources in parentheses within the text and in the order I refer to them:

W—*The Complete Works of Ralph Waldo Emerson*, Centenary Edition, ed. Edward Waldo Emerson (Boston and New York: Houghton Mifflin Company, 1903).

J—*The Journals of Ralph Waldo Emerson*, ed. Edward Waldo Emerson and Waldo Emerson Forbes (Boston and New York: Houghton Mifflin Company, 1909).

I have not used the new and as yet incomplete Harvard Edition of Emerson's journals because it serves my particular purposes no better than the 1909 edition.

Because Emerson's thought was not static and because context is important in his writing, it is helpful to know the dates of his writings and the particular essay from which a statement is taken. Therefore I have appended a list of his works and their respective dates, in the order of the Centenary Edition.

I have tried to acknowledge in the notes all the help I have received from published criticism. In addition I wish to thank four men for their careful consideration of earlier drafts: Joseph Summers, James Colvert, and especially Sherman Paul and Floyd Stovall. Any oversights, faulty reasoning, and indiscretions are my own. I am also grateful to Washington University for two grants that enabled me to complete this book.

The Power and Form of

Emerson's Thought

Chapter I

As Face to Face
The Power and Form of Nature

As EMERSON conceives it, the universe is composed of soul—the "me," or spirit—and nature—the "not me," all that is not spirit (*W*, I, 4–5). Spirit has two characteristics: life in itself and the necessity to manifest itself in material forms (*W*, I, 27, 34–35), which, by implication, do not have life in themselves, but have life by virtue of it. "There is truly but one miracle, the perpetual fact of Being and Becoming, the ceaseless saliency, the transit from the Vast to the particular, which miracle, one and the same, has for its most universal name the word *God*" (*J*, VI, 124). Nature, then, is an effect, the necessary realization of spiritual power, which is not manifold but one (*W*, X, 183, 213; *W*, I, 123).

As an effect, nature is "a projection of God in the unconscious" (*W*, I, 64–65). That is to say, *natura naturans*, the mysterious creative- and life-force in nature, the force that sustains and reproduces living forms according to physical laws, is the mode of activity of spirit as it is transformed or projected into matter, or *natura naturata* (*W*, I, 200; *W*, III, 176, 179, 330). Being unconscious, both the activity of natural forms and the laws of their activity—the physical counterparts of spiritual laws—perfectly obey or express the supreme mind (*W*, I, 197, 199). Thus Emerson rejects the orthodox Christian conception of the sinful condition of nature (*W*, X, 213), and thus he also rejects materialism, the philosophy of Locke accepted by his Unitarian seniors.

His rejection of materialism prompts him to examine its antithesis, idealism. In *Nature* he emphasizes that there is no way we can test the impressions of our senses: we can neither know if we actually perceive something other, nor if that something has substantive existence. Consequently he entertains the idea that perhaps nature is simply an "apocalypse of the mind" (*W*, I, 47–48; see also *W*, I, 332–33). Later Emerson claims, with disarming candor, "the advantage of the ideal theory over the popular faith is this, that it presents the world in precisely that view which is most desirable to the mind" (*W*, I, 59). Some of the implications of this position, however, he cannot accept.[1] For example, just as Lockean materialism implies an

---

[1] Some critics have contended that Emerson adheres to a strict idealism. See

order of stasis—being only—so does its most radical antithesis, subjective idealism, but Emerson sees a dynamic order of becoming, of
development and growth. Also, Emerson too much respects nautral
forms as the manifestation of God to slight their reality, and he respects too much the experience of his senses, which never quite deny
the forms of nature a substantive existence (*W*, II, 13–14): while
vision may be a creative act, the mind and its organs do not create
the object they perceive (*W*, IV, 82). Finally, and most importantly,
he cannot accept the implications of idealism for the substantiality
not only of matter but of man as well.

Yet, if it only deny the existence of matter, it does not satisfy the demands
of the spirit. It leaves God out of me. It leaves me in the splendid labyrinth
of my perceptions, to wander without end. Then the heart resists it, because it balks the affections in denying substantive being to men and
women. Nature is so pervaded with human life that there is something of
humanity in all and in every particular. But this theory makes nature
foreign to me, and does not account for that consanguinity which we acknowledge to it. (*W*, I, 63)

In other words, while idealism may be most desirable to the mind, it
is not desirable to the whole person. Still, Emerson wants some hy-
pothesis that will account for nature by other than materialistic
principles (*W*, I, 62–63) and that will satisfy the mind as well as the
heart.

Even after rejecting idealism he says that nature owes its existence
to spirit, that it is an effect (*W*, I, 49). He also insists that he does not
particularly wish to establish an ontology as such, but to redefine the
relation of man to nature (*W*, I, 59). Keeping these things in mind,
perhaps we find the key to the problem in Emerson's insistence that,
with relation to man at least, nature is a phenomenon (*W*, I, 49, 62),
an object of experience. This insistence implies a sort of idealistic
ontology, vaguely Kantian, which he adhered to from 1836 on, and
the understanding of it clarifies many apparent inconsistencies and
contradictions in his thought.[2]

Joel Porte, *Emerson and Thoreau: Transcendentalists in Conflict* (Middletown,
Conn.: Wesleyan University Press, 1966), chap. 1; Richard J. Blakeney, "Emer-
son and Berkeleian Idealism," *Emerson Society Quarterly* (hereafter cited as
ESQ), No. 58 (1970): 90–97; and Carl Dennis, "Emerson's Poetry of Mind and
Matter," *ESQ*, No. 58 (1970): particularly 146.

[2] Herbert W. Schneider has pointed out, validly in my estimation, that Emerson, among other American writers, is more an existentialist than a phe-
nomenologist, in the strict Husserlian sense of the term "phenomenology." I
am only interested in the fact that Emerson uses the word *phenomenon* carefully and consistently. See "American Transcendentalism's Escape from Phe-

Nature as such is effect, "the rapid efflux of goodness executing and organizing itself," a dynamic order of becoming (*W*, II, 310). The incarnation of God in the unconscious, nature must be regarded as secondary, dependent on spirit, which is primary because it is cause (*W*, I, 56, 57–58, 197). In terms of the whole, nature exists not for its own sake but as a means to an end: "It is the organ through which the universal spirit speaks to the individual, and strives to lead back the individual to it" (*W*, I, 62). And again: "Nature is made to conspire with spirit to emancipate us" (*W*, I, 50; see also *W*, I, 41, 47; *W*, II, 314). In other words, because it is unconscious nature is incomplete. Thus it cannot by itself constitute reality, for reality must include—indeed, it may be a function of—consciousness. One could by implication define nature's goal as becoming conscious. Hence it depends for its fulfillment on spirit in its conscious manifestation as man.

But man depends equally on nature (*W*, I, 42, 95; *W*, X, 132). Without the "not me" he could not become conscious. "That which was unconscious truth, becomes, when interpreted and defined in an object, a part of the domain of knowledge" (*W*, I, 35; see also *W*, II, 335; *W*, III, 196). One cannot say that this truth exists either in nature or in the mind; it is inconceivable without involving both. "He is placed in the centre of beings, and a ray of relation passes from every other being to him. And neither can man be understood without these objects, nor these objects without man" (*W*, I, 27–28). By itself, even though it is real, nature is an apparition, a shadow (*W*, I, 62, 95); by himself man would be no more. Idealism implies as much, and that is why, as we have seen, Emerson rejects it.

At this point the doctrine of correspondence becomes crucial. Without it men would live in a cosmos of private, arbitrary perceptions, a view that Emerson's experience denies. He agrees with the Vedanta that an effect and its cause must have an identity of existence;[3] because man and nature are effects of the same ultimate cause, the mind discovers in nature not merely a handle for any idea but the objective embodiments of particular ideas. "Man carries the world in his head, the whole astronomy and chemistry suspended in a thought. Because the history of nature is charactered in his brain, therefore is he the discoverer of her secrets" (*W*, III, 183). Discovering nature's

---

nomenology," in *Transcendentalism and Its Legacy*, ed. Myron Simon and Thornton H. Parsons (Ann Arbor: University of Michigan Press, 1966), pp. 217–18.

[3] Arthur E. Christy, *The Orient in American Transcendentalism: A Study of Emerson, Thoreau, and Alcott* (New York: Columbia University Press, 1932), pp. 101–2, 104.

secrets involves discovering one's own thoughts (*W*, X, 130); one cannot place the events in a necessary sequence because they are essential aspects of one another. This is not to deny the possibility of mistakes, corrections, or revolutions in thought. The doctrine of correspondence simply states that no valid discovery, application, or communication would otherwise be possible.

Perception is a discovery, not an invention or imposition, and it is grounded in language. In a famous passage Emerson asserts that words signify natural facts, that natural facts signify spiritual facts, and that nature is the symbol of spirit (*W*, I, 25). In itself "deaf and dumb" (*W*, I, 45), nature, a symbol, provides us language; by means of language, also a symbol, we realize the symbolic character of nature, discover the laws of our mind of which, because of correspondence, it is a metaphor (*W*, I, 32). But again, one cannot regard this as a series of events: one cannot conceive of language without consciousness, and one cannot conceive of consciousness without language. By means of language, the creation of symbolic or metaphorical structure, we render unconscious truths conscious, for consciousness is one: "That which intellectually considered we call Reason, considered in relation to nature, we call Spirit" (*W*, I, 27). Therefore the correspondences we discover and embody in language are not arbitrary—they actually exist (*W*, I, 33–34). Furthermore, spirit is by definition creative (*W*, I, 27). Paradoxically, then, through the order of nature we create metaphors, and through metaphors we create the order of nature, for creation is discovery, as the making of metaphor testifies: "It is proper creation. It is the working of the Original Cause through the instruments he has already made" (*W*, I, 31). In the beginning was the Word.

Man and nature cannot be understood without each other, and reality cannot be understood without both, for spirit "does not build nature up around us, but puts it forth through us, as the life of the tree puts forth new branches and leaves through the pores of the old" (*W*, I, 64.) Reality—essence, being—occurs in perception, the transition of nature from the unconscious to the conscious. But we cannot grasp the whole truth, only truths (*W*, II, 304). In the opening paragraph of "Fate" Emerson says, "We are incompetent to solve the times. Our geometry cannot span the huge orbits of the prevailing ideas, behold their return, and reconcile their opposition (*W*, VI, 3). Yet we can only be aware of what we cannot comprehend—orbits, return, and the irreconcilable paradox of planetary opposition—by virtue of our very geometry (and Emerson's metaphorical use of it). In effect, we create greater than we know. Thus perception—that is, reality—is a continuous process that transcends time, becoming that constitutes being and being that constitutes becoming. In the beginning *is* the word: "I am present at the sowing of the seed of the world. With a geometry of sunbeams the soul lays the foundations of nature" (*W*, II, 346). Thus reality is neither spiritual nor material, but a synthesis of the two, a bipolar unity, for "the act of seeing and the thing seen, the seer and the spectacle, the subject and the object, are one" (*W*, II, 269). Or, as he puts it in "Circles," "cause and effect are two sides of one fact" (*W*, II, 314).

"What is a man," Emerson asks, "but nature's finer success in self-explication?" (*W*, II, 352). *Nature's* finer success.[4]

Each form represents the entire order of nature (*W*, II, 340)—"all the aims, furtherances, hindrances, energies and the whole system of every other" (*W*, II, 101)—because each is the product of all the laws of nature, and because all forms are variations of a single property[5]: "I believe this conviction makes the charm of chemistry,—that we have the same avoirdupois matter in an alembic, without a vestige of the old form; and in animal transformation not less, as in grub or fly, in egg and bird, in embryo and man; every thing undressing and stealing away from its old into new form, and nothing fast but those invisible cords which we call laws, on which all is strung" (*W*, VIII, 5; see also *W*, II, 13; *W*, III, 180–81; *W*, VIII, 8–9). This is a monistic position, of course, but law, not a physical atom, is the essence. Reality consists of the orderly dynamic fusion of power and form. Emerson's fascination with the ceaseless flow and metamorphosis of nature reminds one of Thoreau, Whitman, and Louis Sullivan, and he was perceptive enough in his ontological conception of the relation of power and form to agree with Faraday's prediction that, as Emerson puts it, once the "primordial elements" of matter were

---

[4] For an interesting comparison of this metaphysic or epistemology, see Martin Heidegger, *An Introduction to Metaphysics*, trans. Ralph Manheim (Garden City, N.Y.: Doubleday, 1959), especially pp. 156–57, 159–61, 171–73, 183–84, 205. For an interpretation substantially the same see Sherman Paul, *Emerson's Angle of Vision: Man and Nature in American Experience* (Cambridge, Mass.: Harvard University Press, 1952), chap. 3; Charles Feidelson, Jr., *Symbolism and American Literature* (Chicago: University of Chicago Press, 1959), pp. 128–29; Frank T. Thompson, "Emerson's Indebtedness to Coleridge," *Studies in Philology* 23 (1926): 664; Ray Benoit, "Emerson on Plato: The Fire's Center," *American Literature* 34 (1963): 488; James M. Cox, "Emerson and Hawthorne: Trust and Doubt," *Virginia Quarterly Review* 44 (1969): 95; and Lewis Mumford, *The Golden Day: A Study in American Literature and Culture* (New York: Boni & Liveright, 1926), p. 104.

[5] For a good discussion of this point, see Norman Miller, "Emerson's 'Each and All' Concept: A Reexamination," *New England Quarterly* 41 (1968): 381–92.

analyzed, "we should not find cubes, or prisms, or atoms, at all, but spherules of force," and that "under chemistry was power and purpose: power and purpose ride on matter to the last atom" (*W*, VIII, 4–5).[6] Purpose rides with power because the relation of power and form is based on law—in a sense, it is a law—and law implies purpose. Only materialism implies purposelessness.[7]

Because it is ordered and purposeful, nature provides a moral standard or reference for us. Although we are fallen, nature is erect and serves as a differential thermometer (to use Emerson's metaphor) to indicate the presence or absence of the divine sentiment in us (*W*, III, 178). One can claim perfection in nature because we cannot corrupt it (*W*, I, 197); as the projection of God in the unconscious, essentially it is not subject to the human will, its order is serene and inviolable, and thus it remains a fixed point according to which we may measure our departure (*W*, I, 64–65; see also *W*, VIII, 158). It is interesting to note the implicit conception, parallel to the Renaissance conception, of man as God's superior creation, because a conscious incarnation, and yet his consciousness is attained at the compensatory price of will and the consequent liability to sin.

But the idea of nature as a moral reference has not been without its critics. John Stuart Mill makes perhaps the classic attack against Emerson's position (though without specific reference to Emerson) when he states that "nearly all the things which men are hanged or imprisoned for doing to one another, are nature's every day performances," including common torture and murder, and that, even if nature's methods are means to good, they remain bad models for men to follow. In fact, if God is omnipotent, He is evil since He chooses to use for His ends the means of ferocity.[8] To Mill, nature is strictly "red in tooth and claw" and can be used as justification only for rapacious greed, cruel exploitation, and, in general, moral anarchy.

Emerson would have agreed with Mill, as far as he goes, but would have added that Mill's argument stops short. He confines it to a strict

---

[6] Victor Cousin had previously contended that physics had become concerned primarily with forces and laws, and hence he too rejected materialism for "spiritualism." See Octavius Brooks Frothingham, *Transcendentalism in New England: A History* (New York: Harper, 1959), p. 70. Layla Goren has pointed out a significant parallel: "According to the Vedantic teaching, matter is materialized energy, which in turn is an emanation from Brahma, The Creator, that eternal essence that is the innermost Self of all Things." *Elements of Brahmanism in the Transcendentalism of Emerson*, in *ESQ*, Supplement to No. 34 (1964): 23.

[7] See Alfred North Whitehead, *Science and the Modern World* (New York: Macmillan, 1931), pp. 157–58.

[8] *Three Essays on Religion* (London, 1923), pp. 28, 31, 37.

observation of the behavior of forms, without considering the laws of power. Emerson is aware of the ferocity in nature, and he insists that we are not to act according to the guiding sentiment of natural law by imitating that ferocity—are not to use that ferocity to justify our own—because we have a moral organization superior to the rest of nature: "The excellence of men consists in the completeness with which the lower system is taken up into the higher—a process of much time and delicacy, but in which no point of the lower should be left untranslated; so that the warfare of beasts should be renewed in a finer field, for more excellent victories" (*W*, X, 189; see also *W*, IV, 11; *W*, XI, 155). In terms of literal behavior, accordingly, what is moral for the rest of nature may be immoral for us. But to perform a moral act we must follow the same laws of lower nature, translated onto higher planes of meaning. It is the laws of nature that Emerson intends as a moral reference: "The laws of moral nature answer to those of matter as face to face in a glass" (*W*, I, 32–33). Mill's argument fails because it restricts itself to the literal behavior of forms and does not take into account both the laws of which that behavior is a manifestation and the translatability of those laws onto higher planes. The laws, understood properly, Emerson considers to be a valid reference because they are moral, that is, they work toward universal good (*W*, X, 85–86).

We can perceive the laws of nature and translate them onto a moral plane of meaning because, once again, of correspondence.[9] As necessary manifestations of spirit, forms have a spiritual character, a spiritual significance that corresponds with their progenitor, we can translate the physical laws onto higher planes, and therefore the laws of the material, intellectual, and moral realms govern within their respective spheres in corresponding ways (*W*, VIII, 222–23; *W*, X, 183). "Intellect and morals appear only the material forces on a higher plane" (*W*, X, 72; see also *W*, IV, 83). It is largely in this sense that nature serves as a discipline for us.

A good example of such a translation is Emerson's doctrine of compensation, based on the polarity one finds throughout nature—inhalation and exhalation, ebb and flow, motion and rest, man and woman, odd and even, spirit and matter, and so on—and the inherent balance in nature it implies, each pole balancing the other so that an equitable mean, in time, is inherently maintained (*W*, III, 194–95; *W*, II, 96–98).

One of the most important manifestations of polarity is cause and effect. Despite the argument of Hume, showing that we can only

---

[9] An influence on this point was Œgger. See Régis Michaud, *Autour d'Emerson* (Paris: Bossard, 1924), p. 98. See also Bliss Perry, *Emerson Today* (Princeton, N.J.: Princeton University Press, 1931), p. 82.

observe succession and not connection among phenomena, Emerson contends for connection: "We are natural believers. Truth, or the connection between cause and effect, alone interests us." He takes this position on psychological and pragmatic grounds: whether we can see it or not, we believe a connection exists, because it is the basis of order (*W*, IV, 170). "It is necesary to suppose that every hose in Nature fits every hydrant; so only is combination, chemistry, vegetation, animation, intellection possible. Without identity at base, chaos must be forever" (*W*, XII, 20). When an event in nature seems to contravene her own law of cause and effect, we are deceived by our own ignorance; with greater knowledge we would see that no violation actually occurs. (*W*, III, 181). Not to believe in cause and effect is the basis of genuine scepticism (*W*, VI, 220). As Hume himself recognizes, we are natural believers, naive or not. Emerson feels that we are not, because scepticism—distrust of the permanence of the laws, if not actual disbelief in the laws—would paralyze our faculties and lead eventually to self-annihilation (*W*, I, 48). If we implicitly believe in cause and effect as a natural law, why not as a moral law? In his doctrine of compensation, Emerson attempts to justify this belief.

The basis of order is the identity of existence in cause and effect. As Arthur Christy explains: "Both Karma and Compensation represent the counterpart of the physical law of uniformity in the moral world. They are the laws of the conservation of moral energy as well as physical energy in a world where there is nothing uncertain or capricious."[10] In other words, one unavoidably reaps what one sows. Therefore true justice is irresistibly meted to us, here and now in this world, by the very order of reality (*W*, II, 102–3). It does not pay not to be good, since each evil act effects an immediate diminution of one's soul, one's moral or proper self. The punishment is contained as seed in the crime itself. The punishment is the price to be paid, and a price is exacted of everything that is not of the soul: every material good has its tax, every material misfortune its benefit. We pay for the cultivation of certain faculties with the neglect of others. Worldly success implies a neglect of moral values; on the other hand, cultivation of moral values often hinders worldly success. In our lives we can expect calamities, but calamities also provide the

[10] *The Orient in American Transcendentalism*, pp. 101–2, 104. Henry Bamford Parkes has pointed out the resemblance (actually, in Parkes's view, the identity) of Emerson's doctrine to Jonathan Edwards's principle of contrast. *The Pragmatic Test: Essays on the History of Ideas* (San Francisco: The Colt Press, 1941), p. 34.

opportunity—perhaps necessity is a better word—for spiritual growth. Enduring them, one may (one may have to) emerge a finer person (*W*, II, 98–99, 122, 124–25). "Every thing has two sides, a good and an evil," but this does not imply a doctrine of indifference, because underlying or transcending the realm of everything is the soul, or being itself, the whole. "Nature, truth, virtue, are the influx from thence. Vice is the absence or departure of the same" (*W*, II, 120–21). The wicked, by their acts, diminish their being, while of the virtuous no price is or can be exacted because each of their acts is an affirmation of the soul, an addition of being, "the incoming of God himself, or absolute existence, without any comparative" (*W*, II, 121–22).[11] We could say that polarity is a dialectical process in the realm of forms, of becoming; and performing a virtuous act, while elevating the actor into the transcendent realm of power, of being, is paradoxically a part of the process.[12]

In his doctrine of compensation Emerson attempts to indicate (not prove, as he points out) the correspondence of natural and moral law. Natural forms, being incarnations in the unconscious, involuntarily obey natural law, whereas man, being conscious, must voluntarily obey moral law (*W*, X, 55; *W*, VI, 240; *J*, V, 560). The obedience of natural forms exemplifies the relationship of the two basic constituents of nature—power, in its manifestation as physical law, and form —a relationship we can call organic. Emerson's conception of organicism reflects to a great extent the work of Goethe (whom Emerson studied closely), who coined the very word *morphology* and helped replace Linnaeus's generic concept with the modern genetic concept of the formation and transformation of organic forms, thereby shifting biological interest from the classification and products of life to the processes of life.[13] Emerson finds the organic concept congenial

[11] On this point, see Kenneth Burke, "Acceptance and Rejection," *The Southern Review* 2 (1937): 606.

[12] Jonathan Bishop indicates that a problem still remains, that of compensation for the victim of a calamity, such as a fatal accident. Emerson's response, as we shall see, could have been his stoicism, but since he himself never relates it directly to compensation, Bishop's objections are well founded. See *Emerson on the Soul* (Cambridge, Mass.: Harvard University Press, 1964), p. 75. See also Henry F. Pommer, "The Contents and Basis of Emerson's Belief in Compensation," *PMLA* 77 (1962): 248–53, and Roland F. Lee's very acute analysis, "Emerson's 'Compensation' as Argument and as Art," *New England Quarterly* 37 (1964): 291–305.

[13] Ernst Cassirer, *Rousseau, Kant, Goethe: Two Essays*, trans. James Gutmann, Paul Oskar Kristeller, and John Herman Randall, Jr. (Princeton, N.J.: Princeton University Press, 1947), pp. 68–69.

because it takes into account a world of becoming as well as a world of being; it defines a dynamic rather than a static order.[14]

The relation of power and form is organic in that the forms of nature are productions or expressions of divine faculties, of power (*W*, VIII, 43). And natural forms are beautiful because they perfectly express divine faculties: in their structure they precisely answer their end without outside embellishment, which Emerson regards as deformity (*W*, VI, 290; *W*, XII, 160–61). Their perfection is a basic assumption, as one can readily infer from the way various writers— Carlyle, Thoreau, Sullivan—develop the aesthetic implications of the organic theory, so classically defined by Coleridge:

The form is mechanic, when on any given material we impress a predetermined form, not necessarily arising out of the properties of the material;—as when to a mass of wet clay we give whatever shape we wish it to retain when hardened. The organic form, on the other hand, is innate; it shapes, as it develops, itself from within, and the fulness of its development is one and the same with the perfection of its outward form. Nature, the prime genial artist, inexhaustible in diverse powers, is equally inexhaustible in forms;—each exterior is the physiognomy of the being within.[15]

Emerson insists that all beauty must be organic (*W*, VI, 290), and he defines true beauty as "the instant dependence of form upon soul" (*W*, III, 3), which precludes any extraneous embellishment. Organisms are an aesthetic ideal because they perfectly express nature's power, their own essence. A plant, in short, grows out of its own seed, and the process and result of its growth are the outcome of the laws of the seed.

The implications of the organic idea are not just aesthetic. From a different perspective Coleridge explains the concept as individuation, the impulse of all forms of life progressively to fulfill or realize their own nature.[16] As self-existence is a basic attribute of the supreme

[14] Richard Adams argues "that the fundamental impulse of romanticism was the shift from staticism to dynamism, and that organicism was mainly a means of control, a defense against chaos, and a technical resource for writing, rather than an article of belief." "Permutations of American Romanticism," *Studies in Romanticism* 9 (1970): 250–51. Adams's argument is wonderfully provocative, but needs the correction, it seems to me, that for Emerson at least organicism was an article of belief, a means of control that was more than a technical resource, it was a truth.

[15] *Lectures upon Shakespeare and Other Dramatists*, ed. Mrs. H. N. Coleridge, vol. 4 in *The Complete Works of Samuel Taylor Coleridge*, ed. W. G. T. Shedd (New York: Harper, 1853), p. 55.

[16] *Miscellanies, Aesthetic and Literary: to which is added The Theory of Life*, ed. T. Ashe (London: George Bell, 1911), p. 391.

cause, so it is of lower forms: "Power is, in nature, the essential measure of right. Nature suffers nothing to remain in her kingdom which cannot help itself" (*W*, II, 70–71). In a Leibnizian sense, existence as such—the realization of the organism's essential nature, or individuation—is good,[17] but there is an additional emphasis on progressive realization or growth. Power here means physical power, but Emerson is careful to state that such power is always right in nature, not among men. The beauty of natural forms stems from their perfect realization of natural power, but Emerson feels that men need a new doctrine of forms, because "there is no accurate adjustment between the spirit and the organ [i.e., the individual], much less is the latter the germination of the former" (*W*, III, 3). With self-reliance—a moral translation of the physical law describing the relation of power and form—Emerson hoped to contribute a new doctrine of forms.

The law becomes moral, of course, because it is not involuntarily obeyed. Unlike the forms of nature, we are endowed with consciousness, the moral sentiment, and free will. With these faculties we can either act in harmony with the great tendency to individuation or can, within ourselves, thwart it (*W*, X, 91–92). Lower organisms fulfill themselves through physical power, but because we have consciousness, we must fulfill ourselves through self-existence expressive of the conscious moral sentiment, the end of which is the attainment of a state of virtue, or character (*W*, X, 99, 114). To perform the virtuous act a man must obey the moral sentiment, not assert his private will, must act for the good of the whole, not for himself. He gives himself up to, and thereby incurs an addition of, being. Thus Emerson can claim that self-reliance means finally not egoism but reliance upon God (*W*, II, 69–70; *W*, X, 65–66; *W*, XI, 236). As we shall see, with the doctrine of self-reliance Emerson is in large part attempting to redefine humility in modern, viable terms.[18]

Another aspect of the dynamic relation between power and form is the fact that forms are not rigid, but are in a state of constant flux or change: each form germinates, grows, matures, decays, and dies. Considered in terms of the whole economy of nature, and within the

[17] In this respect, and in his attitude toward the relationship between God and man, Emerson's conception of God's goodness parallels that of Augustine, Pseudo-Dionysius, and Aquinas as well as Leibniz, "goodness" referring more to God's creative energy and fecundity than to his redemptive grace. See Arthur O. Lovejoy, *The Great Chain of Being: A Study of the History of an Idea* (New York: Harper, 1960), pp. 179–80, 67.

[18] For a most provocative argument of the younger Emerson as egoist, see Quentin Anderson, *The Imperial Self: An Essay in American Literary and Cultural History* (New York: Knopf, 1971), chap. 1.

context of boundless space and time, forms evolve in an ascending progression: the life-force "publishes itself in creatures, reaching from particles and spiculae through transformation on transformation to the highest symmetries, arriving at consummate results without a shock or a leap" (*W*, III, 179). The ascension of forms involves another ancillary law, which is a variation of power and form, the law of evolution.[19]

Emerson sometimes describes nature as self-existent, "always circular power returning into itself" (*W*, I, 85), and he confesses that such a view is not compatible with an evolutionary doctrine (*J*, VIII, 86). Perhaps the difficulty stems from the relation of the infinite to the finite; that is, the creator, being itself, is above or outside of space and time, and yet the creation is in space and time—in a state of becoming. Reconciling the two, as A. O. Lovejoy has shown, has proven to be one of the supreme problems of philosophy and theology. In any case, in terms of the temporal order, Emerson always conceived of a unitary power publishing itself through a myriad of forms in constant flux or change. And he was thoroughly imbued with the organic idea that each form expresses its essential power through growth. He simply had to connect the organic concept of growth with the Neo-Platonic doctrine of flux—expanding the idea of growth from the individual organism to the entire organism of nature—to derive a purposive or teleological pattern of progressive transformation of forms, expressing an ascending power, to have an evolutionary doctrine (*W*, I, 372; *W*, III, 24).[20]

The question remains, does the connection work? Richard Adams has cogently argued that it does not, that the concept of organicism in and of itself involves a fatal contradiction: "The contradiction lies between the assertion of an ultimately perfect organic unity, which must necessarily be static, and the assertion of a continually changing dynamic diversity which, because it continues to change, cannot be either perfect or unified. Emerson insisted on having it both ways, in spite of the contradiction."[21] And, as we have seen, in spite of his own confession of incompatibility. Yet Emerson does insist, in the faith (it seems to me) that ultimately the relation between the two—being and becoming, power and form—is not contradictory, but para-

[19] For a different point of view on this doctrine, see Joseph Warren Beach, "Emerson and Evolution," *University of Toronto Quarterly* 3 (1934): 479, 488.

[20] Richard D. Mosier entitles the Transcendentalist conception of God "evolutionary theism." To the Transcendentalist, the proof of God "lay in the process of growth itself." *The American Temper: Patterns of Our Intellectual Heritage* (Berkeley and Los Angeles: University of California Press, 1952), pp. 189, 191.

[21] "The Basic Contradiction in Emerson," *ESQ*, No. 55 (1969): 106–7.

doxical. Adams's argument, while it may be metaphysically correct, assumes a sufficiency of reason (in the common sense of the term) that Emerson denies. Consistently he can only account for existence, in the whole and in its parts, as involving eternity and time: "These roses under my window make no reference to former roses or to better ones; they are for what they are; they exist with God today. There is no time to them. There is simply the rose; it is perfect in every moment of its existence. Before a leaf-bud has burst, its whole life acts; in the full-blown flower there is no more; in the leafless root there is no less. Its nature is satisfied and it satisfies nature in all moments alike" (*W*, II, 67). As with the roses, so with the universe: deny time and we deny the incontrovertible fact of flux; deny eternity and we deny the equally incontrovertible fact of ordered flux, the roses' pattern of growth, the universe's pattern of evolution.[22]

Emerson also accepted the doctrine of evolution—in a teleological, rather than Darwinian, form—because he saw, as few contemporaries did, that it could serve as an essential corroboration of a religious view of life. It is interesting to note that Whitehead shares this view, explaining that an evolutionary philosophy is inconsistent with materialism because matter as such can only change; it cannot evolve. Evolution implies progression, qualitative meaningful change, which the principles of materialism deny. Evolution also implies a single underlying activity or energy (or power) expressing itself in nature's manifold progression. "Thus in the process of analyzing the character of nature in itself, we find that the emergence of organisms depends on a selective activity which is akin to purpose."[23] Emerson regards the doctrine of evolution as a perfect corollary to the organic theory, thereby dispelling the conception of a mechanistic universe with the conception of a vitalistic universe.

He cites the doctrine as a gracious lesson which conspires with the principle of faith and hope, in that the process is progressive, moving from simple to complex structure (*W*, XI, 525–26). The lower races that are extinguished are necessary for the development of the higher; this is one purpose of ferocity (*W*, X, 188; *W*, VI, 35–36), and it introduces the consideration that Emerson believes evolution to be

[22] Hence Carl Strauch asserts that Emerson's "bringing emanation and evolution together is the most ambitious and fruitful manipulation [a word about which I have reservations] of his system of polarity." "Emerson as Literary Middleman," *ESQ*, No. 18 (1960): 6.

[23] *Science and the Modern World*, pp. 157–58. Harry Modean Campbell points out the similarity of Emerson's and Whitehead's views on this point: "Emerson and Whitehead," *PMLA* 75 (1960): 581. For another comparison of Emerson and Whitehead, see Charles L. Sanford's "Emerson, Thoreau, and the Hereditary Duality," *ESQ*, No. 54 (1969): 36–39.

not just physical, but moral as well: "Nature is a tropical swamp in sunshine, on whose purlieus we hear the song of summer birds, and see prismatic dew-drops—but her interiors are terrific, full of hydras and crocodiles. In the pre-adamite she bred valor only; by and by she gets on to man, and adds tenderness, and thus raises virtue piecemeal" (*W*, X, 188). One possible implication Emerson never confronts directly is that God Himself is in the process of evolution, is growing, and therefore is not omnipotent but limited. We must then say that God is doing His best. The phrase may indicate why Emerson never troubles himself with the idea.

One implication, however—an implication of all the natural laws as well as of evolution—he did confront, and from 1844 on he paid it particularly close attention. Because of their absolute uniformity and regularity, natural laws provide us with order, but at a compensatory price: "Nature does not cocker us; we are children, not pets; she is not fond; everything is dealt to us without fear or favor, after severe universal laws" (*W*, III, 159; see also *W*, III, 64). In 1841 he pointed out that while nature's basic law is amelioration, or evolution, toward benefit, it must be understood that the benefit is for the whole, without the least preference for any of the individual forms (*W*, I, 200–1). No one can dismiss calamity as exceptional, because what has happened once can happen again and must be feared (*W*, VI, 8); nor is physical pain exceptional but inherent in the order of nature (*W*, VI, 19). The order is grand yet terribly inconvenient: "It may be styled a cruel kindness, serving the whole even to the ruin of the member" (*W*, I, 373). Emerson sums up the general disposition of nature best, perhaps, when he describes it as no sentimentalist in its prodigious creation and destruction of forms (*W*, VI, 6).

Life consists of power and form, and the excess of either is the cause of physical harm, according to Emerson's depiction of mankind's attitude toward destiny:

The word Fate, or Destiny, expresses the sense of mankind, in all ages, that the laws of the world do not always befriend, but often hurt and crush us. Fate, in the shape of *Kinde* or nature, grows over us like grass. We paint Time with a scythe; Love and Fortune, blind; and Destiny, deaf. We have too little power of resistance against this ferocity which champs us up. What front can we make against these unavoidable, victorious, maleficent forces? What can I do against the influence of Race, in my history? What can I do against hereditary and constitutional habits; against scrofula, lymph, impotence? Against climate, against barbarism, in my country? I can reason down or deny every thing, except this perpetual Belly: feed he must and will, and I cannot make him respectable. (*W*, IV, 177)

On the one hand we can regard as physical harm the unavoidable, inherent limitation of the individual's freedom, the restrictive tyranny of organization or form over power, such as low intelligence, a weak constitution, etc. (*W*, VI, 8–9, 10–11, 19–20). On the other hand we can define physical harm as the excess of power, or ferocity: a common means of self-expression, or survival, that is inherited in a surplus of the passions, of sexual instinct, hunger, and thirst (*W*, VII, 324–25). The surplus of these characteristics composes part of the inherited tendency toward individuation, the basic impulse of all life: each form strives to grow in its own direction as far as possible, and in the midst of inevitable conflicts to maintain, by whatever means nature provides, its own law of being against other creatures (*W*, IV, 28). It is this impulse of self-direction that ultimately maintains the equilibrium of nature (*W*, III, 236; *W*, VII, 276), and without the attendant violence, there would be no efficiency, no progression in survival. Without electricity, Emerson says, "the air would rot" (*W*, III, 185).

Thus the excess of power proves to be, in fact, a paradoxical indication of the goodness of the laws responsible for the behavior of forms. It marks the instinct of self-help, the effort of forms at all risks to attain for themselves their being (*W*, XI, 154–55). This attitude of Emerson's amounts to a variation on the doctrine of the fortunate fall; we prefer being or fulfillment earned to fulfillment given. Fulfillment given, in fact, is a contradiction in terms. In the evolutionary process, ferocity among lower forms simply indicates the vitality necessary for progression to higher forms; it does not detract from nature's universal aim of benefit (*W*, X, 188–89; *W*, VI, 35–36).

Emerson insists that a force is always at work to make the worst good and the best better (*W*, XI, 486), but this suggests a possible contradiction: for the individual forms, physical harm and pain are fatal, yet amelioration is also fatal (*W*, VI, 35–36): "Let us build altars to the Blessed Unity which holds nature and souls in perfect solution, and compels every atom to serve an universal end" (*W*, VI, 48). If there is such a compulsion, we may not be free, and the order of nature would have no moral significance.

Emerson attempts to resolve this crucial issue by distinguishing between fate and necessity:

Our doctrine must begin with the necessary and eternal, and discriminate Fate from the necessary; there is no limitation about the Eternal. Thought, Will, is co-eternal with the world; and, as soon as intellect is awaked in any man, it shares so far of the eternity,—is of the maker, not of the made. But Fate is the name we give to the action of that one eternal, all-various necessity on the brute myriads, whether in things, animals, or in men in whom the intellect pore is not yet opened. To such it is only a burning wall which hurts those who run against it. (*J*, IX, 216)[24]

He defines necessity as law for the benefit of all, whereas "in destiny, it is not the good of the whole or the *best will* that is enacted, but only *one particular will*. Destiny properly is not a will at all, but an immense whim" (*W*, XII, 408). Only to the brute myriads does necessity appear to be fate; thought transforms fate into necesity, and after doing so can risk the paradox that freedom is necessary (compare *Paradise Lost*, wherein God foreordains man's free will): upon the perception of necessity we must choose whether to live in accordance with it or not (*W*, VI, 23, 48–49, 240). Like Goethe and Schiller,[25] Emerson is suggesting that freedom and necessity are correlative, even concomitant, ideas; it is freedom and destiny or freedom and fate that are opposed.

In the same way, John Hospers distinguishes between casuality and compulsion—respective equivalent terms for Emerson's necessity and destiny—and his analysis helps clarify that of Emerson and his contemporaries (and predecessors). An event that occurs according to the law of cause and effect occurs necessarily because a law is, by definition, exceptionless. Compulsion, however, is something over and beyond causality; it implies, as Emerson says of destiny, lawless whim. In Hospers's words, "if the presence of certain characteristics are what entitle an act to be called 'compelled,' then the absence of those same characteristics entitle it to be called 'uncompelled,' or free. Freedom is the opposite of compulsion, not of causality."[26] The necessity Emerson speaks of actually means uniformity, the law by which events occur, and is actually the antithesis of whim, or compulsion. And whim, or compulsion, is antithetical to freedom: were nature lawless, totally unpredictable, choice would prove meaningless, futile, absurd. Necessity, therefore, is not incompatible with freedom; rather, it is a prerequisite for it. And because natural law, or necessity, in the corresponding human realm becomes moral, man's freedom is moral: "nothing is free but the will of man, and that only to procure his own virtue: on every other side but that one he beats the air with his pompous action" (*J*, III, 423; see also *W*, X,

---

[24] As Carl F. Strauch indicates, Emerson's conception here parallels that of Proclus, who differentiates between the law for matter, or fate, and the law for intellect, or providence. See "The Importance of Emerson's Skeptical Mood," *Harvard Library Bulletin* 2 (1957): 129–30.

[25] See Cassirer, *Rousseau, Kant, Goethe*, p. 91.

[26] *An Introduction to Philosophical Analysis* (Englewood Cliffs, N.J.: Prentice-Hall, 1954), pp. 269–70, 272–73.

208). A man procures his virtue by voluntary obedience to the necessity he perceives; in that choice, to obey or not, lies his essential freedom as Emerson defines it (*W*, VI, 240). This definition, incidentally, does not represent a delimitation of an earlier notion of freedom. In *Nature* Emerson says that conceiving of man as the creator in the finite "animates me to create my own world through the purification of my own soul" (*W*, I, 64). Other times he says as much; always he implies it (see, e.g., *W*, I, 41, 73, and "The Divinity School Address"). By freedom, Emerson never means that one can do anything one wishes.

Man's freedom is moral, yet according to Emerson's law of necessary amelioration, one serves universal ends willingly or not. But he also indicates that this law, which always brings things right and turns evil to good, gives a man no excuse for ignoring moral imperatives, for duty requires him to act, here and now, as the agent of this law (*W*, X, 189; see also *W*, X, 232–33). He must do this, not to help the evolution of the world, which is beyond his power to injure, but for the sake of his own soul. As a moral being, he fulfills himself by adhering to the world order, which is moral.

At this point Emerson may seem to contradict himself. The laws work for the benefit of the whole, and yet their impartial regularity and consistency cause the physical and suffering of individual forms. But this is simply a fact of compensation; if the good of the whole were not maintained, individual forms could not benefit nor indeed survive. Emerson further contends, however, that although the laws are impartially beneficial, individual persons are "dear to the heart of being" (*W*, VII, 132; *W*, II, 293). The problem in human terms resides in the meaning of benefit.

> There is this eternal advantage to morals, that, in the question between truth and goodness, the moral cause of the world lies behind all else in the mind. It was for good, it is to good, that all works. Surely it is not to prove or show the truth of things,—that sounds a little cold and scholastic,— no, it is for benefit that all subsists. As we say in our modern politics, catching at last the language of morals, that the object of the State is the greatest good of the greatest number,—so, the reason we must give for the existence of the world is, that it is for the benefit of all being. (*W*, X, 91)

The benefit we find in nature is the possibility it provides, in Sherman Paul's words, of "spiritual aggrandizement,"[27] of moral growth through service to the moral law, obedience to the moral sentiment, and thereby the attainment of a state of virtue (*W*, VII, 275; *W*, V,

---

[27] *The Shores of America: Thoreau's Inward Exploration* (Urbana, Ill.: University of Illinois Press, 1958), p. 8.

247). God's order is good primarily as a moral order, and only secondarily as an order conducive to physical comfort.

In fact, the moral order derives from the very regularity and impartiality of natural laws that cause physical harm and discomfort. According to this line of thought, concisely developed by F. R. Tennant, a modern theologian, we cannot have an order primarily moral and primarily conducive to comfort at the same time. Freedom depends on necessity, the laws of nature; so does consciousness. And morality depends on freedom and consciousness: they are all aspects of one another. If the regularity of these laws causes physical pain, Tennant argues that such pain is a concomitant of a moral cosmos, a necessary consequence of a particular (and the best) kind of order. (The basic question of ethics is not, is man happy, but how does man deserve to be happy?) We should not construe physical ills as bad "because they are parts of an order which subserves the highest good in providing opportunity for moral developement [*sic*]. And they are not superfluous ills because they are the necessary outcome of that order."[28] Emerson, as we have seen, also asserts the incompatibility of a cosmos primarily moral and primarily comfortable, and he gives to the laws of nature the same moral role. Hence his stress on our natural and necessary faith in them: we base our lives entirely on this implicit perfect faith, for without it we would be paralyzed and would inevitably find ourselves in the midst of moral anarchy—an end that Emerson, being a moralist, deplores above all (*W*, I, 48; *W*, XII, 20). To prevent such anarchy he gives the great burden of responsibility to us.

Because he rejects the doctrine of innate depravity, Emerson places all moral responsibility on each individual (*J*, VI, 502; *W*, III, 76). As a practical result of this responsibility, the only real harm that can happen to one must come from oneself (*W*, II, 123). Real harm, as he explains in "Compensation," refers to the soul, that is, choosing to act in such a way that one diminishes one's being. Because the individual soul is the whole, that which serves the good of the whole—which Emerson calls the right—serves also the good of the individual (*W*, X, 197).

With regard to physical pain and suffering, therefore, the individual should realize that the world is not constituted for his self-indulgence, but for its own catholic ends, which he should make his own (*W*, X, 84). The balance of good in the tabulation of brute facts,

---

[28] *Philosophical Theology* (Cambridge: Cambridge University Press, 1930), 2: 199–200, 201–2. Tennant differs from Emerson, however, in denying that physical harm and pain are means to good.

though small, is always there, and it represents the beneficent tendency of power on which Emerson bases his optimism. Men find it difficult to recognize this beneficence because they are normally selfish, narrow, and thereby short-sighted (*W*, I, 371–72). When looking at forms from a nonegocentric view, one sees that all loss and pain are particular, and that the universe, being, remains essentially unharmed. Only in the finite realm of form is there suffering; the infinite realm of power always exists in a state of self-contained repose (*W*, I, 74; *W*, II, 131–32). Pain is relative, serene repose absolute, and it is in the perception of the absolute that we truly exist, or exist most profoundly, in power rather than merely in forms (*W*, I, 57). And with the perception of the absolute comes what Emerson considers the very height of culture and behavior: "the identification of the Ego with the universe." Simultaneously, we understand the difference between the private temporal self and this ego, the impersonal soul, being within and without (*W*, XII, 62). This identification and distinction compensates the individual for his private suffering, for "he is to rally on his relation to the Universe, which his ruin benefits. Leaving the daemon who suffers, he is to take sides with the Deity who secures universal benefit by his pain" (*W*, VI, 47). In fact, given a true identification, the individual cannot really be ruined.

This is the essence of humility, the basic conclusion of many religious thinkers, and a conclusion Emerson always comes to: "And the blindness of the intellect begins when it would be something of itself. The weakness of the will begins when the individual would be something of himself" (*W*, II, 271; see also *W*, I, 122, 124). In lower nature there is no such consciousness; forms unconsciously work for the good of the whole, without choice, and therefore the "not me" cannot be debauched. The individual, on the other hand, must choose to fulfill his universal, not his private, consciousness and thereby serve the whole:

> I confess that everything connected with our personality fails. Nature never spares the individual; we are always balked of a complete success: no prosperity is promised to our self-esteem. We have our indemnity only in the moral and intellectual reality to which we aspire. That is immortal, and we only through that. The soul stipulates for no private good. That which is private I see not to be good. "If truth live, I live; if justice live, I live," said one of the old saints; "and these by any man's suffering are enlarged and enthroned." (*W*, VIII, 342–43)

With such an attitude, reminiscent of Carlyle, Emerson could have extended his doctrine of compensation to the victim of calamity, although he never explicitly did so.

Emerson's solution to the problem of physical pain is stoic: by trusting in the serene, inviolable, beneficent order of the whole, we can cope with all the evil that it contains and uses for its own ends. Indeed, "we cease to care for what it will certainly order well" (*W*, X, 193).[29] We cease to care, but not indifferently, and not only for the suffering of others, for Emerson desires that we be willing to "perish, and perish gladly, if the law remains" (*W*, X, 195). His attitude, then, is generally consistent with that of Seneca—that man possesses a rational nature (Emerson would say a soul, intuitional as well as rational) in common with the power that creates and rules the cosmos. By identifying his good with its good, the individual places himself above circumstance, transforms fate into Providence, and thereby can calmly suffer any evil, indeed, can perish gladly.[30]

This doctrine of a stoical self-reliance, as Emerson defines it, does not imply an anarchic isolation of individuals one from the other; rather, in accordance with the law of polarity translated into a higher plane of meaning, it finally implies a social orientation. As Coleridge succinctly explains the paradox, "this tendency to individuate cannot be conceived without the opposite tendency to connect, even as the centrifugal power supposes the centripetal, or as the two opposite poles constitute each other, and are the constituent acts of one and the same power in the magnet."[31] Emerson's organic view of nature includes a cooperation concomitant with self-reliance, for each organic form, in order to grow and survive, requires the harmony of massive physical forces (*W*, X, 70, 83): a blade of grass is the journeywork of the stars. By implication, the balance that characterizes nature requires the successful growth and existence of individual forms.

In the same manner, the individual needs society and culture for his development, and he should therefore apply whatever he has developed for society's benefit (*W*, VII, 15–16). The most important mode of development, furthermore, is moral, and the most significant aspect of self-reliance is its moral orientation; seen as reliance upon God, it results finally in the man of virtue: "All the virtues are special directions of this motive; justice is the application of this good of the whole to the affairs of each one; courage is contempt of danger in the

[29] For an interesting comparison, see Josiah Royce, *The Religious Aspect of Philosophy: A Critique of the Bases of Conduct and of Faith* (Boston: Houghton Mifflin, 1885), p. 451.

[30] Edmund Grindlay Berry, *Emerson's Plutarch* (Cambridge, Mass.: Harvard University Press, 1961), pp. 9–10.

[31] *Miscellanies*, p. 391.

determination to see this good of the whole enacted; love is delight in the preference of that benefit redounding to another over the securing of our own share; humility is a sentiment of our insignificance when the benefit of the universe is considered" (*W*, X, 92–93). Society requires self-reliance for without such individuals it can never become basically good (*W*, III, 265–67). Social alienation as the consequence of a genuine self-reliance indicates the evil condition of society. One should not conform to it, but should, as much as possible, point the way to the moral law. "Whoso would be a man, must be a nonconformist. He who would gather immortal palms must not be hindered by the name of goodness, but must explore if it be goodness. Nothing is at last sacred but the *integrity* of your own mind" (*W*, II, 50–my italics). Paul makes much the same point: "And be not conformed to this world; but be ye transformed by the renewing of your mind, that ye may prove what is that good, and acceptable, and perfect, will of God (Rom. 12:2).[32] Self-reliance serves thereby a social end. This is the harder way, Emerson insists—harder than conformity—but society is part of the whole that one should prefer to the private self.

With all his emphasis on morality, Emerson needs some criterion for gauging good and evil in the flesh. The relationship of power and form in nature, when translated into the realm of moral values, allows him to look at the scale of being from above or below, ideally or historically, respectively: "We say Paradise was; Adam fell; the Golden Age, and the like. We mean man is not as he ought to be; but our way of painting this is on Time and we say *was*" (*J*, IV, 287).[33] The doctrine of evolution poses no obstacles in interpreting the scale either way, for the power is transcendent and the means are historical (*J*, VI, 497). In the context of time, or evolution, we have a basis of judgment and of hope: "Remark the unceasing effort throughout nature at somewhat better than the actual creatures: *amelioration in nature*, which alone permits and authorizes amelioration in mankind. The population of the world is a conditional population; these are not the best, but the best that could live in the existing state of soils, gases, animals, and morals: the best that could *yet* live; there shall be a better, please God" (*W*, I, 372–73). By translating evolution into a moral

[32] A parallel indicated by Jerry A. Herndon, "St. Paul and Emerson's 'Self-Reliance,'" *American Transcendental Quarterly* 1 (1969): 90.

[33] Michael H. Cowan discusses the way Emerson uses metaphors that simultaneously idealize and describe, and thereby measure the actual by the ideal. See *City of the West: Emerson, America, and Urban Metaphor* (New Haven and London: Yale University Press, 1967), pp. 20, 26–27.

doctrine, one can judge men by a conditional or relative standard, from the standpoint of form, or by an absolute standard, from the standpoint of power.

The two standards of evaluation are not contradictory: having intelligence and a conscious moral sense, we are responsible here and now for our moral condition. The difference lies in the forms our morality takes. Radoslav Tsanoff has offered a "gradational" theory of evil that is helpful in clarifying this point, as indeed it is helpful in understanding all of Emerson's ethic. According to this theory, evil is essentially self-degradation, the surrender to impulses that are lower in the scale of being than we. It is necessarily only relative to good. Tsanoff quotes Augustine: "When the will abandons the higher, and turns to what is lower, it becomes evil, not because that is evil to which it turns, but because the turning itself is perverse." Paradoxically, evil unresisted, willingly embraced, becomes evil absolute.[34] And we must turn the paradox around: the order we live in being evolutionary, virtue involves incessant growth, aspiration toward higher and higher levels; self-satisfaction at any one level devolves into stagnation, if not regression. Emerson says that a true state of mind rested in becomes false (*W*, II, 339): the same is true of a mode of action or a state of being.[35]

The attainment of character, in correspondence with evolution, occurs by growth. Because of his finite nature the individual can grow infinitely in that he cannot attain perfection, and hence he should ceaselessly strive for improvement (*W*, II, 316–17; *W*, VII, 275). Emerson defines the essential act of life as "transition, shooting the gulf"—nature ceaselessly striving, as men should, to better itself (*J*, VIII, 501). Accordingly, at one stage of an individual's life an act can be moral that later would be immoral (*W*, X, 184–85; *W*, XI, 166–67). But at any particular stage, his participation in a particular act that is at that point moral creates a perfect harmony between his soul and the moral law: he is virtue (*W*, II, 122; *W*, XII, 417). But he cannot rest there: transition is the essential act of life. Because of this method of evaluation, Emerson is able to praise a certain set of attitudes and activities, such as prudence, from one moral level, and from a higher level, such as heroism, find it inadequate, even immoral. It all depends on the moral level of the individual performing the act.[36]

---

[34] *The Nature of Evil* (New York: Macmillan, 1931), pp. 392–401.

[35] On this same point, see Henry D. Gray, *Emerson: A Statement of New England Transcendentalism As Expressed in the Philosophy of Its Chief Exponent* (Stanford, Calif.: Stanford University Press, 1917), p. 73.

[36] This relative and hierarchical method of ethical evaluation accords with Kenneth Burke's clarification of the way Emerson views nature. From here

He applied the same evaluation to mankind as a whole: a certain moral attitude in one society may in another, more advanced or enlightened, be immoral. Hence he never reprimanded ancient Greece for its system of slavery, but found that institution in nineteenth-century America to be totally depraved. The "gradational" morality proved extremely valuable to Emerson in his examination of society and civilization, for it helped him keep his mind receptively appreciative of social differences and development, and it provided him a useful basis and means of evaluating his own society.

---

and now, so to speak, Emerson reveres nature as a means to the end of transcendence, union with God; from the vantage point of that transcendence he can almost despise it as inferior, illusory. "I, Eye, Ay—Emerson's Early Essay 'Nature': Thoughts on the Machinery of Transcendence," in *Transcendentalism and Its Legacy*, pp. 18–19. Burke's interpretation also clarifies the apparently contradictory ways in which Emerson regards aesthetic form.

Chapter II

A Middle Measure
The Power and Form of Society

IN THE BROADEST SENSE Emerson's conception of society is organic. Ernst Cassirer's definition of Rousseau's social theory (and ideal) defines Emerson's as well: the social bond, he explains, "must bind together freely acting persons, not dead things. Hence it cannot be something imposed upon the wills of these persons from without; they must constitute and create it themselves."[1] This conception is romantic, of course, because at base it is a type of subjectivism: the social bond should express the inner condition of its participants. Romanticism, however, also can mean a different type of subjectivism, not organic, but willful.

Aware of this ambiguity in meaning, Emerson attempts to distinguish as sharply as possible between the two kinds of subjectivism, calling the organic classic and the willful romantic. Drawing an analogy between art and society, he explains that whereas romantic art and social institutions are the products of inclination, whim, and caprice, classic art and institutions are organic, the products of inherent necessity and law, expressive of the deepest needs and beliefs of their creators (*W*, XII, 303–4). One distinguishes between the two, as we have seen, by the ends sought: the former involves a concern merely for private, the latter for universal ends, even at the expense of the private. Although Emerson's terminology may be strange, his meaning is clear: he defines himself as an organicist.

Nature is the general expression of spiritual power, and particular natural organisms are expressions of their own life-force. Analogously, the various institutions composing society embody those ideas accepted by a sufficient number of people so that they become what may be called social thoughts, and the vitality and value of those thoughts depend on their basis in morality (*W*, XI, 160–61; *W*, VII, 32–33). Emerson considers morality, because it is necessary for a civility of a high order, to be the true end of society, the institutions to be the forms of it and the means to it; and the social power, when it is moral, is the proper kind of power, for it is then in harmony with universal law (*W*, VII, 26; *W*, XI, 309–10). Therefore, just as Ruskin insists that justice, not utilitarian expediency, is the only valid basis

[1] *Rousseau, Kant, and Goethe*, p. 31.

for enduring institutions, Emerson claims that forms that are the product of moral ideas are actually the most practical:

Governments have their origin in the moral identity of men. Reason for one is seen to be reason for another, and for every other. There is a middle measure which satisfies all parties, be they never so many or so resolute for their own. Every man finds a sanction for his simplest claims and deeds, in decisions of his own mind, which he calls Truth and Holiness. In these decisions all the citizens find a perfect agreement, and only in these; not in what is good to eat, good to wear, good use of time, or what amount of land or of public aid each is entitled to claim. (*W*, III, 212–13)

This statement, out of context, makes it appear that Emerson contends that social forms are necessarily the result of moral force; they are, but only at a certain time in their history. Thus he hopes (without predicting) that, as its contribution to history, America will make its laws, institutions, governments, and economy the dynamic, enduring embodiments of the moral sentiment (*J*, X, 144). Because social power is properly intellectual and moral, however, usually only a small minority of the populace subscribes to it. Those who do not he can dismiss as the mass. He feels that a society should be judged qualitatively, by its best representatives, not by the majority (*W*, III, 229–30; *W*, VI, 248–49; *W*, VIII, 216–17).

Because the power that creates institutions is intellectual, and because ideas change, social forms are no more fixed, rigid, or static than the evolving forms of nature (*W*, III, 199); the rise and adoption of new ideas cause their modification and disappearance (*W*, II, 302). "Epoch after epoch, camp, kingdom, empire, republic, democracy, are merely the application of his manifold spirit to the manifold world" (*W*, II, 4). Change is inevitable, because manifold man is himself in a constant state of change; consequently, to be efficacious, a form must embody an idea people believe in. "We are superstitious, and esteem the statute somewhat: so much life as it has in the character of living men is its force. Our statute is a currency which we stamp with our own portrait: it soon becomes unrecognizable, and in the process of time will return to the mint" (*W*, III, 200; *W*, X, 111–12). The inevitability of and necessity for change are of course one more ramification of the organic mode of thought.

Using religious forms as an example, Emerson explains that truths concerning human nature and laws relating to conduct are received through revelation. In nature, there is a necessity for spirit to embody itself in forms; so in society the seer attempts to embody the truths and laws in outward forms, to preserve for himself a specific remembrance of his revelation and to stimulate others to follow it. The result is the church. The institution, then, is an end of the vision and a simultaneous means of implementing it. The revelation and the church depend for their continuing validity on the presence of the spirit that created them. Forms alone, however, are insufficient for transmitting the ideas and sentiments responsible for them from individual to individual or from age to age, for spirit is, by definition, ever creative. No one revelation is the last. Hence each person must create his own forms, and each age its own, which does not rule out the possibility of accepting those existing forms genuinely expressive of the particular spiritual state of the individual or the age. The form, in short, is necessary, but by itself inadequate.[2]

We see quite clearly how Emerson regards the relationship of social power and social forms in his description of the reform movement of the mid-nineteenth century as, in fact, "the continuation of Puritanism, though it operate inevitably the destruction of the church in which it grew, as the new is always making the old superfluous" (*J*, VI, 53). Often, as in this instance, the new makes the old superfluous only in a formal sense, for the ends sought—truth, moral rectitude, justice—remain the same. As a contemporary of Emerson's, Orestes Brownson, expresses it, "The [religious] sentiment is lodged in the bottom of the soul, always the same, unalterable, and eternal; the form is variable and transitory."[3] On the other hand, change as such is not necessarily good. Hence Emerson's constant challenge to build American forms on the foundation of ethics: "The constitution and law in America must be written on ethical principles, so that the entire power of the spiritual world can be enlisted to hold the loyalty of the citizen, and to repel every enemy as by force of Nature" (*W*, X, 111). Ideally, then, society depends upon moral social ideas and vital forms that are true implementations of those ideas. Both are necessary and desirable; together they constitute an ideal middle measure, the perfect balance of power and form.

In agreement with Theodore Parker, Orestes Brownson, and Wilhelm Dilthey, Emerson believes that because social ideas change, particular social forms should be evaluated according to a relative scale: "We may be wise in asserting the advantage in modern times of the democratic form, but to other states of society, in which religion consecrated the monarchical, that and not this was expedient. Democracy is better for us, because the religious sentiment of the pres-

---

[2] *The Early Lectures of Ralph Waldo Emerson*, ed. Stephen E. Whicher, Robert E. Spiller, and Wallace E. Williams (Cambridge, Mass.: Harvard University Press, 1964), 2: 92–93.

[3] "Benjamin Constant," in *The Transcendentalists: An Anthology*, ed. Perry Miller (Cambridge, Mass.: Harvard University Press, 1950), pp. 85–86.

ent time accords better with it. Born democrats, we are nowise
qualified to judge of monarchy, which, to our fathers living in the
monarchical idea, was also relatively right" (*W*, III, 207). No specific
form is right or wrong as such, but is right or wrong relative to the
social power of the time. Accordingly, democracy suits the religious
sentiment of Americans because of the supreme value they place on
each individual (*W*, XI, 258). In any case, the prevailing form of
government, right or wrong, indicates the level of culture in the
population that permits it (*W*, III, 200).[4]

We may take the extent of belief in an idea as the indication whether or not it is a social thought, and the intensity of belief as the measure of the idea's social power. Great ages require widespread devout
belief in spiritual truth (*W*, VI, 216). The measure of the value of a
form, on the other hand, is its use (*W*, XI, 23). According to Emerson, a form should truly express the power underlying it, and serve
as an effective means of communicating that power to others. As
Theodore Parker says: "Religious forms may be useful and beautiful.
They are so, whenever they speak to the soul, and answer a want
thereof."[5] Emerson thinks that in Asia, for example, the institution
of caste arises naturally and properly out of the deep belief in a fate
deaf, relentless, and immense (*W*, IV, 52). He says that at one time
Calvinism was right: he calls it "an iron belt to the mind, giving it
concentration and force," and in his journal he describes it as "the
breath of a hot village of Teutonic peasants, exalted to the highest
power, their notions of right and wrong ... their notions of law and

---

[4] Compare Orestes Brownson's statement of the same conception: "All past
social institutions have had and fulfilled their mission. They are not to be
tried by the present, but by that epoch in the progress of society to which they
belonged. Tried by this standard, most of the institutions which we now
condemn, will be found to have been good in their day, and the evil which is
charged against them belonged, not to their origin, but resulted from their
lingering too long, from their outliving their time." "Progress of Society," in
The Transcendentalists, p. 92. Dilthey, in his analysis of historical relativism,
also asserts an ideal of balance: "As every shape which historical life takes is
finite there must be a balance of joyful power and pressure, of expansion and
narrowness of existence, of satisfaction and want. Its fundamental tendency
reaches the height of effectiveness for a short time only." *Pattern and Meaning
in History: Thoughts on History and Society*, ed. H. P. Rickman (New York:
Harper, 1961), pp. 156–57. Dilthey differs importantly from Emerson in rejecting
"a super-empirical subject manifesting itself in the individual consciousness"
(p. 154), but he does posit something like a common mind all men share (pp.
67–68).

[5] "A Discourse of the Transient and Permanent in Christianity," in *The
Collected Works of Theodore Parker*, ed. Frances Power Cobbe (London:
Trübner, 1864), 7: 5.

punishment and reward" (*W*, X, 204; *J*, X, 242). But that form, like the form of caste, did not suit the social ideas of nineteenth-century America. Emerson insists on a relativistic and pragmatic mode of evaluating social forms.

One social ideal Emerson emphasizes, however, and one he feels the American people discovered is that only that state can endure which recognizes an injury to the least member as damage to the whole (*W*, XI, 352); or, to state the proposition in the obverse form, the highest politics is for the state to work for the greatest good of the greatest number (*W*, VII, 34). This conviction does not necessitate any specific forms, because people may differ in their notion of the good. But it does require, especially in a democratic society, a balance of power and forms in the sense that the forms can accommodate the differences among men. The sanity of society, Emerson asserts, must result from the balance of the thousand insanities of its members (*W*, I, 384–85; *W*, III, 237).

With his conception of power and form Emerson has a specific means of evaluating any society. The basic question concerns the expression of the conscience, or the moral sentiment, of the period. "Is the age we live in unfriendly to the highest powers; to that blending of the affections with the poetic faculty which has distinguished the Religious Ages?" (*W*, XI, 391–92). This question enables one to judge whether the forms of society are satisfactory or unfit in relation to the power therein. Forms do reflect, indeed even help mold, social ideas, and thus indicate the level of culture in a society. Yet on the other hand, forms can be wrong. For example, judging from contemporary institutions, Emerson found his countrymen, in comparison to the preceding Calvinists, to be frivolous, ungirt, foppish (*W*, X, 203–4). "Our culture is very cheap and intelligible. Unroof any house, and you shall find it. The well-being consists in having a sufficiency of coffee and toast, with a daily newspaper; a well-glazed parlor, with marbles, mirrors, and centre-table; and the excitement of a few parties and a few rides in a year.... Our civility, England determines the style of.... It is that of a trading nation; it is a shop-keeping civility" (*W*, XI, 123). Because the end of shopkeeping was commerce and profit, this civility, he continued, condoned exploitation and slavery. The institutions in this case were an unfortunate indication of the peculiar power of the people, and by his criteria of judgment Emerson could logically condemn, as he often did, both the power and the forms: "We in America are charged with a great deficiency in worship; that reverence does not belong to our character; that our institutions, our politics, and our trade have fostered a self-reliance which is small, liliputian, full of fuss and bustle." Believing only in the senses and the understanding (the lower, prudential, rational faculty), he continued, "our imagination and our moral sentiment are desolated" (*W*, X, 206-7). Here the poor institutions accurately reflected the deficient character of the people, and both needed to be reformed. If, on the contrary, the institutions should not reflect the social character, should they for example be vestiges from a previous age thwarting the enactment of contemporary moral values, they alone would need to be changed.

The problem of determining which type of reform is necessary rests not in the criteria, but in the application of the criteria, the determination itself. The fact is, people disagree whether something should be done or not, and what and how much should be done. Emerson sees this disagreement as basically two-sided, between the conservative and the liberal, the party of the past and the party of the future, of memory and of hope; the division reflects the polarity of nature (*W*, I, 295-96). Each side has its own basis in truth; conservatism takes its stand on necessity, liberalism on ethics. Conservatism looks at the world historically, and believes the present to be the cumulative result, the best that nature could yet create or is yet possible. Liberalism looks at the present idealistically, from the viewpoint of the moral sentiment and thereby accuses the past and the present and requires the impossible of the future. And Emerson pinpoints the strength of the conservative position: "although the commands of the Conscience are *essentially* absolute, they are *historically* limitary" (*W*, I, 301-2).

The world is not an illusion, and in the view of the conservative any attempt to transcend its limitations—the tendency of the reformer—must not only fail, but must react harmfully against the reformer because he himself is a part of it. The existing world is a sacred fact: "This also was true, or it could not be: it had life in it, or it could not have existed: it has life in it, or it could not continue" (*W*, I, 303). As Ruskin, Taine, and Sullivan were later to say, the world is what it is because of no one voluntarily and purposefully, but of all; it is the result of the existing degree of culture in the populace (*W*, I, 313).

Moreover, so deep is the foundation of the existing social system, that it leaves no one out of it. We may be partial, but Fate is not. All men have their root in it. You who quarrel with the arrangements of society, and are willing to embroil all, and risk the indisputable good that exists, for the chance of better, live, move, and have your being in this, and your deeds contradict your words every day. For as you cannot jump from the ground without using the resistance of the ground, nor put out the boat to sea without shoving from the shore, nor attain liberty without rejecting obligation, so you are under the necessity of using the Actual order of things, in order to disuse it; to live by it, whilst you wish to take away its life. The past has baked your loaf, and in the strength of its bread you would break up the oven. (*W*, I, 304–5)

Emerson appreciates and respects the conservative position, the position aligned with form, the party of Must as opposed to May. But he feels that its limitation, its partiality, stems from its failure to recognize that one aspect of Must is a man's instinct to rise and to love and help his fellow man (*W*, XI, 231–32). Must alone is insufficient, for May is as much a necessity in life as Must, is itself an aspect of Must.

Liberalism involves looking at forms from the point of view of ethics, or conscience, comparing the idea and the fact (*W*, I, 271). Theodore Parker feels that Emerson clearly sees the disparity between the institutions that represent man's history and the ideas that come of his nature, and that his effort is to encourage each individual to do his part to connect the two realms of being.[6] For it is in this effort alone that man progresses, because of the nature of the effort: "the origin of all reform is in that mysterious fountain of the moral sentiment in man, which, amidst the natural, ever contains the supernatural for men. That is new and creative. That is alive. That alone can make a man other than he is. Here or nowhere resides unbounded energy, unbounded power" (*W*, I, 272). Men who are selfishly concerned merely for possession strive to retain the status quo, so that it is necessary for men of intelligence and virtue to stimulate new ideas and higher ideals that will result in better forms; in so doing, not only are special abuses checked, but the conscience and intellect of the people are educated (*W*, XI, 241; *W*, I, 269).

Emerson, of course, is liberal, a reformer, but he does not wish to be "absurd and pedantic" to the extent of alienating himself from society altogether, for that can effect no improvement (*W*, I, 247). Both positions—the conservative and the liberal—by themselves run to ridiculous extremes. Conservatism is noncreative, entirely mnemonic; it always attempts to maintain the status quo, believes in a negative fate, has no faith in the ability of men to govern themselves, distrusts principles and therefore nature. "Reform in its antagonism inclines to asinine resistance, to kick with hoofs; it runs to egotism and bloated self-conceit; it runs to a bodiless pretension, to unnatural refining and elevation which ends in hypocrisy and sensual reaction." Emerson, we can see, is just as clearly aware of the dangers of liberalism run mad as Hawthorne and Melville. Since each position alone

---

[6] *Ibid.*, 10: 252.

ends in dangerous irrelevance, Emerson's attempt, as usual, is to re-concile them. Each is a good half, true as far as it goes, but is an impossible whole, so that in a true, or ideal, society and in a true man both must be combined (*W*, I, 298–99). This balance or fusion of the two is better because it accurately reflects the polarity of which reality is composed, and wisdom is the result. "Wisdom does not seek a literal rectitude, but an useful, that is a conditioned one, such a one as the faculties of man and the constitution of things will warrant" (*W*, I, 302). In other words, the organic theory of society, as Emerson develops it, serves not only as a description of society, but as an ideal as well: the true society is a balance of power and form—a middle measure—for an excess of either is harmful. Because much in society is harmful, there is disproportion; society is often, perhaps usually, a flawed organism, and by far the most common flaw, as Emerson sees it, is an excess of form.[7]

In many instances, people live according to forms whose original in-tellectual impulse has died, vestiges from an earlier period in which they were useful and true, or pragmatically valid, but have now lost their truth, or vitality (*W*, X, 105–6; *J*, IX, 174–75). Forms are essential, but adherence to a form after it is outgrown is unreasonable, and, in a religious context, unchristian (*W*, XI, 20–21). With regard to the Catholic Church, for example, Emerson can agree with the heart and motive, the truth or sentiment, of the great fathers, but he is discontented with the limitations, the surface, the language, the expression of their insights. Their statement is for him as fabulous as Dante's Inferno (*W*, X, 227). For in religion the principles are immortal, but the expression of them—the institution, the theology—needs constant modification and change (*W*, X, 108). Whitehead makes precisely the same point, and for precisely the same reasons. "This evolution of religion," he explains, "is in the main a disengage-ment of its own proper ideas from the adventitious notions which have crept into it by reasons of the expression of its own ideas in terms of the imaginative picture of the world entertained in pre-vious ages." As the picture of the world changes through scientific discovery, so should the statement of religion. "If the religion is a sound expression of truth, this modification will only exhibit more adequately the exact point which is of importance. This process is a gain."[8] It is a gain and therefore works to the advantage of religion, but only if religion distinguishes between, in Theodore Parker's phrase, "the transient and the permanent," and if it is properly receptive to the discoveries of science, rather than blindly resistant.

But the rigid adherence to dead forms is apt to involve such a resistance, because these forms are completely insulated from the real concerns of life and business at the time, thereby making religion irrelevant (*W*, I, 139). Such forms, originating from without instead of within, are inconsistent with vital experience and help induce resistance to it (*W*, XI, 488). In the same way, the American fondness for importing foreign forms, Emerson observes, not only expresses but stimulates a triviality of purpose that contradicts the true end of society, to make us better men: these forms, that is, divorce us from the real issues of life (*W*, XI, 533).

Dead forms or imported forms unsuited to our use confine and check the growth of the mind: "A sect or party is an elegant incognito devised to save a man from the vexation of thinking" (*W*, XI, 18, 478; *J*, II, 386). And men are all too ready to be so saved, ready to accept uncritically the religions and politics they inherit (*W*, VIII, 248). "We are too easily pleased" (*W*, VII, 125). Men often find it easier to achieve congenial association on the basis of their weaknesses and faults rather than their strengths and virtues; the society whose forms encourage such association lowers rather than elevates them (*W*, VII, 13). Society as a whole, moreover, encourages a passive attitude; because of its quest for stability, it conspires against the manhood of all its members, as witness the typical parental desire for the child to repeat the elder's life. "You are trying to make that man another *you*. One's enough" (*W*, II, 49–50; *W*, X, 137–38). Society, in other words, attempts to perpetuate its forms after they are no longer useful, thereby reinforcing its members' inclination to accept forms of vestigial usefulness.

Nor is it just the perpetuation of dead forms that creates the problem, but an exclusive reliance on form as such, dead or alive. Of the two constituents of polarity, effect is worthless when separated from its cause. Reliance must be placed on the cause-in-the-effect, on both together, lest the cause be lost sight of altogether, but we tend to adhere to the effect and forget the cause (*J*, IV, 270). "I think there never was a people so choked and stultified by forms. We adore the forms of law, instead of making them vehicles of wisdom and justice" (*W*, XI, 258). Therefore, the very aim of government, as Emerson conceives it, can be self-defeated, as the issue of slavery made apparent. With the federal fugitive slave law in mind, he stressed that even in Massachusetts, where all the public forms were right men were not safe and free. "Why? Because the judges rely on the forms, and do not, like John Brown, use their eyes to see the fact behind the forms" (*W*, XI, 270–71). And the reason for the ugly fact behind the forms was that their origin and purpose had been forgotten.

Another aspect of the same problem is the tendency to confuse means for ends:

> The horseman serves the horse,
> The neatherd serves the neat,
> The merchant serves the purse,
> The eater serves his meat;
> 'T is the day of the chattel,
> Web to weave, and corn to grind;
> Things are in the saddle,
> And ride mankind.
>
> There are two laws discrete,
> Not reconciled,—
> Law for man, and law for thing;
> The last builds town and fleet
> But it runs wild,
> And doth the man unking.
>   (*W*, IX, 77–78)

Like Carylye and Ruskin and Marx, Emerson believes that in an industrial society, when the best political economy—the care and culture of men—is lost sight of, the machines unman their users, and the individual workers degenerate into mechanical functionaries without general power. With a change of fashion and demand whole towns are sacrificed, and men are ruined because they are no longer proper individuals, capable of thinking and choosing to apply their talent to new labors (*W*, V, 167–68). The Greeks, in their love of forms, were unaware, Emerson notes, of the evil excess such a formalism can lead to: "They saw before them no sinister political economy; no ominous Malthus; no Paris or London; no pitiless subdivision of classes,—the doom of the pinmakers, the doom of the weavers, of dressers, of stockingers, of carders, of spinners, of colliers" (*W*, IV, 53). Industry and commerce are not intrinsically unfit or evil, but when confused as ends they become vitiated by the derelictions and the abuses of which all are guilty, and the contagion spreads to other professions and practices, into the whole institution of property, until the laws establishing and protecting it, which should be the result of a desire for justice and the good of the whole, become the issue instead of selfishness and greed (*W*, I, 230–31, 233–34). And the contagion is not checked by a religion that is excessively formal.

Religion, as we have seen, can be too formal through a perpetuation of dead forms. But it can also be too formal in the sense we are discussing now, the sense of too much reliance on forms alone, the effect exclusive of the cause. The churches are built on the idioms of Christ's language, the figures of his rhetoric, on his tropes instead of his principles, and in focusing on these forms alone God is considered, in effect, as dead, thus depriving forms that otherwise would be satisfactory of their potential value (*W*, I, 129, 134). Punctuality replaces faith, good taste replaces character: people lose an energetic, vigorous virtue by too much refinement, by a Christianity entrenched in establishments and forms. Every Stoic was a Stoic, but where in Christendom, Emerson asks, is the Christian? (*W*, X, 205; *W*, II, 85).[9]

To Emerson the test of a form is its usefulness; therefore, when believers and unbelievers live in an identical manner, when their practical mores are the same, he distrusts the religion (*J*, X, 43). And if there is no real difference in the way they live, it is because an excessively formal religion has a separate existence, distinct from all other experiences. Thus it only intensifies the tendency to confuse means and ends and further the consequent dehumanization of life, evident in the political economy (*W*, X, 199). Men must be wary of the effect (often dangerous) forms have on character.

Adherence to lifeless forms and lifeless adherence to forms potentially alive induce a shallow, impoverished effeminacy, induce cant, perjury, and hypocrisy, all derivative of the divorce between religion and morals attendant upon a mindless formalism. People become godless and mechanized, without bonds of fellow feeling, without enthusiasm, no longer men, but embodied appetites, passions, and diseases (*W*, X, 229; *W*, V, 228–29, 230; *W*, VI, 207–8). And it then becomes possible, even probable, to profess a religious faith and simultaneously indulge in practices condemned by that faith. This disparity between profession and practice is one of Emerson's deepest concerns:

if you combine it [Christianity] with sharp trading, or with ordinary city ambitions to gloze over municipal corruptions, or private intemperance, or successful fraud, or immoral politics, or unjust wars, or the cheating of Indians, or the robbery of frontier nations, or leaving your principles at home to follow on the high seas or in Europe a supple complaisance to tyrants,—it is a hypocrisy, and the truth is not in you; and no love of religious music or of dreams of Swedenborg, or praise of John Wesley or of Jeremy Taylor, can save you from the Satan which you are. (*W*, XI, 289–90)

[9] For a similar analysis of Emerson's discontent with conventional formal religion, see Harold Fromm, "Emerson and Kierkegaard: The Problem of Historical Christianity," *Massachusetts Review* 9 (1968): 743–44.

Emerson was specifically afraid that the corruption in American politics had gone beyond a reasonable limit, and that consequently the country was composed primarily of men recklessly and exclusively concerned for their aggrandizement (*W*, X, 86).

The effect of mass conformity is to extinguish a genuine individualism by closing off all the channels of inspiration from God to man, and the consequence is a general death of faith (*W*, XI, 534; *W*, I, 135). Men of ability, of intellectual and artistic promise, through the effect of property, degenerate into selfish, petty housekeepers; they succumb to forms so far as to risk the integrity of their personal character for the sake of acquiring the external authority of some office. They join the "devil's party," not realizing that they cannot turn at pleasure from good to evil and back again to good. The corruption spreads to the people, who then condone official injustice and, by using the forms themselves, and in the same way, become inextricably enmeshed in the involuted toils of this evil (*W*, X, 355; *W*, XI, 519–20; *W*, VIII, 232–33; *W*, XII, 317; *W*, I, 234). The result can be a paradoxical inversion: the people's character becomes inferior to some of the society's better forms. "*Representative Government* is really misrepresentative; *Union* is a conspiracy against the Northern States which the Northern States are to have the privilege of paying for" (*W*, XI, 259). The better forms, in fact, can be betrayed by the social power.

Emerson observed that Americans had tried to hold together two states of civilization: a higher state, in which labor, land tenure, and the right of suffrage were democratic; and a lower state, in which the old military tenure of prisoners or slaves, and of power and land in the hands of a few, were oligarchical. The lower had corrupted politics, public morals, and social intercourse in America for many years (*W*, XI, 298–99). Americans had disregarded the moral law, had ignored, or even worse, condoned an exception to the Bill of Rights. But the moral law, the nature of things, could never be safely ignored: the violation had poisoned the body politic and, Emerson warned, if not purged, would destroy it (*W*, XI, 352).

It is equally dangerous to ignore the moral implication that secular progress, the evolution of man to his highest powers, brings with it not only "the gift of sensibilities," but the obligation of higher duties that the will of society must fulfill (*W*, XI, 299). Tolerance of the adherence to forms so outgrown as to be now flatly wrong dulls men's moral sensibilities to the extent that they no longer have a sense of right—organs and glands take precedence over intelligence and the principles of culture and progress (*W*, XI, 229).

The degrading effect of slavery, for example, extended to those responsible for the system. It made the owners slaves to their system, Emerson believed, filled them with vices, informed their children with pride and sloth and sensuality, deprived their women of their proper role, and robbed them all of any genuine security. Moreover, slavery itself became for the holder not a means to an end—that of wealth and luxury—but an end in itself: "But I think experience does not warrant this favorable distinction, but shows the existence, besides the covetousness, of a bitterer element, the love of power, the voluptuousness of holding a human being in his absolute control" (*W*, XI, 125, 118). When the form becomes the end rather than a means, forms that should have been superseded mold the social power, to the extent that they truly become expressive of the power.

For the fact was, Emerson charged, American institutions coincided with the spirit of the age, actually sprung from the people's ruling passions, so that the superficial forms were the true images of superficial wants, indicating the American citizen's ugly, ungoverned temper, his brief and shallow affections, and his base sort of hope (*W*, III, 207–8; *W*, VII, 56–57; *W*, XI, 165). In a context larger than America, yet compatible with American values, Emerson considered the spirit of the age to be materialistic, the aim being sensual success or wealth, and English institutions to be the perfect embodiment of this proprietary passion (*W*, IV, 224: *W*, V, 164). Likewise, American institutions embodied selfish drives, reflected the contraction of ethics to the very narrow duty of paying debts, demonstrated the low worship of prudence and convenience, and revealed, in general, the lack of any interest in excellence, truth, or justice (*W*, I, 232; *W*, X, 62–63; *W*, VII, 111; *W*, XI, 385).[10] The proof that existing forms and the true interests they embodied were so bad lay, Emerson said, in the presence and prevalence of fear: "Fear is an instructor of great sagacity and the herald of all revolutions. One thing he teaches, that there is rottenness where he appears. He is a carrion crow, and though you see not well what he hovers for, there is death somewhere. Our property is timid, our laws are timid, our cultivated classes are timid. Fear for ages has boded and mowed and gibbered over government and property. That obscene bird is not

[10] Compare Emerson's indictment of American life with that of Alexis de Tocqueville, who found the basic philosophy in America to be "self-interest rightly understood," and indicated that it was an attitude that led not to an inclination to self-sacrifice or high idealism, but to petty ambitions and an abiding regard for comfort, with the likely result of a stability of mediocrity. *Democracy in America*, ed. Phillips Bradley (New York: Random House, 1960), 2: 130–31.

there for nothing. He indicates great wrongs which must be revised" (*W*, II, 111–12).

It could now seem that Emerson is involved in endless contradiction, at least as here interpreted. At one point power outgrows forms, necessitating their change and development, yet men in society are inclined to consolidate existing forms and resist the necessary change. At another point blind adherence to forms stultifies power, so that the forms come to reflect the spiritual condition of the people. The dilemma is easily resolved by recalling the distinction between the private and the universal consciousness or ego, which Emerson claims never to have confused (*J*, VII, 431). Forms are suitable when they are expressions of the higher concern—the concern, that is, with the moral law—of the universal ego, to which we should subordinate our private or biographical egos. The idolatry of forms, on the other hand, results in a sole concern with the personal interests of our biographical egos, and in that case, the forms, though needing change in relation to our moral nature, are an accurate reflection of the dominance of our inferior interests. But the presence of fear testifies that we cannot deny the moral sentiment, or the moral law of which it is a part, with impunity. Forms, then, can simultaneously be—and this is really not a paradox—inadequate images of our spiritual nature, which has been submerged, and truthful images of our existing interests. It is at this point in Emerson's thought that we can understand his dissatisfaction with conventional reformers.

Emerson always sympathizes with the sentiment desiring reform because it arises from the conviction in an innate worthiness in men that will respond to worthy ideals (*W*, I, 248–49). He also believes that a mere change of forms alone is insufficient to stimulate that innate worthiness (*W*, I, 149–50). The common fault of reformers, as he sees it, is that they try to improve social conditions by concentrating solely on such an external change, rather than concentrating directly on men themselves, and the basis of this fault lies in a weakness or error of perception: "The great majority of men, unable to judge of any principle until its light falls on a fact, are not aware of the evil that is around them until they see it in some gross form, as in a class of intemperate men, or slaveholders, or soldiers, or fraudulent persons." They take a single manifestation as the embodiment of all evil, and bend all their efforts to remedying it (*W*, I, 279). Like Hollingsworth and Ahab, they see only partially, and hence their remedies are partial, pitting against a wrong association another association, against masses more masses. Emerson has a constant fear that the means used to achieve reform might injure, indeed, even replace, the true ends of the reformers; for, in that case, the reform movement would acquire the very faults of the institutions that need to be reformed (*W*, III, 263, 261). By using the external means of money and parties and by employing and exploiting fear, anger, and pride reformers belie their professed belief in the inner life. They mix with the pure energy of the moral sentiment personal and party passions and measureless exaggerations and as a consequence prefer some pet measure to justice and truth (*W*, I, 276–77).

The mixture of the moral sentiment with personal and party passions usually results in fanaticism, the desire to destroy some one thing at any cost, the erection of a special benefit into a panacea (*W*, I, 214–15). This is a fatal partiality, because it comes so far short of the true mark: "Do not be so vain of your one objection. Do you think there is only one? Alas! my good friend, there is no part of society or of life better than any other part. All things are right and wrong together. The wave of evil washes all our institutions alike." One can play the game of life, to use one of Emerson's metaphors, with the existing counters just as well as with new ones, because as long as individual men are not renovated, society gains little or nothing by a merely formal change; new counters alone will not change the game (*W*, III, 261–62).

The problems of the system of private property illustrate precisely Emerson's objection to conventional methods of reform. In his view, both those for and against the status quo are agreed on the supreme value of property, either as owners or enviers. No one (as Paul Goodman has also complained) is really on the other side, able to provide an insight into the problems of property and to propose meaningful solutions, because everyone is either trying to keep or trying to get (*J*, VI, 128; *W*, IV, 256; see also *W*, I, 388). Therefore people will, even after a change of forms, retain the values of the old system, as has consistently happened in the past: "Piracy and war gave place to trade, politics and letters; the war-lord to the law-lord; the law-lord to the merchant and the mill-owner; but the privilege was kept, whilst the means of obtaining it were changed" (*J*, VII, 430; *W*, V, 174). Fraud simply replaces force, and capitalists have the same power of life and death over workers that the feudal lords had over churls (*W*, X, 328). Emerson's analysis, we see, coincides with that of Marx, but he could never have agreed to Marx's plan of remedy, for to him the past clearly demonstrates that the devil can get along comfortably in any institution (*W*, XI, 234).

Conventional reformism—even of the most radical sort—Emerson regards as actually only a mask under the cover of which a more terrible reform, which no one dare name, which dare not name itself,

advances (*J*, VII, 205). Whether actually advancing or not, this reform is terrible because essential, and difficult because it requires the
recognition of a bitter ethical fact: "There is no virtue which is final;
all are initial. The virtues of society are vices of the saint. The terror
of reform is the discovery that we must cast away our virtues, or
what we have always esteemed such, into the same pit that has con-
sumed our grosser vices" (*W*, II, 316–17). Emerson, in other words,
insists that a genuine reform, *the* reform, must occur in the realm of
power.

The way genuinely to improve imperfect forms is to elevate purpose among the people (*W*, VII, 117). The better society is to be
made not out of foolish, sick, and selfish men, such as they now are,
but by men transfigured, raised by the power of principles above
themselves (*W*, I, 250–51). Men must make morals the test of forms
and of themselves, and Emerson expresses the hope for a new church
founded on a moral science exact enough to become the algebra and
mathematics of ethical law, inducing a religious attitude and practice more stern and exigent than any stoicism (*W*, X, 114; *W*, VI,
241). And the essential sentiment of morals to apply to reform is love,
a power ultimately more effective than force. When love and severe
ethics are the rule, just concessions to the poor will be granted by the
rich rather than seized from them, and only then will a true revolution
have occurred: man will have exchanged, according to Emerson's
imagery, his marketcart for a chariot of the sun (*W*, I, 253–54; *W*,
VI, 215). Such a reform may be millennial, but Emerson insists that it
alone would be of enduring value, or would even endure.

There is no doubt, however, that Emerson, in his reaction against
conventional methods and aims of reform, sometimes goes too far
in the opposite direction, unrealistically slighting the importance of
forms in daily living, and lets his millennial obscure his practical
vision. When he says that a slave elevated by the religious sentiment
is no longer a slave, he may be right in terms of power, but this is
small consolation to a man owned by another (see *W*, I, 280–81).
However properly concerned over the fact that a man can be a slave
without the institution of slavery, in his irritation with the abolition-
ists for overlooking the essential problem of man's inner freedom he
simply ignores the importance of abolishing the institution, ignores
his own awareness of the effect forms can have on character.

His irritation can also lead him into an exaggerated rhetoric of
rejection, as for example the passage in "Self-Reliance" in which he
angrily denounces philanthropy and charity, declaring the dollar
he occasionally contributes, out of weakness, "a wicked dollar" (*W*,

II, 52). His anger is not utterly antihumanitarian; rather, he is against the sort of charity that perpetuates the conditions it is supposed to alleviate, which serves primarily to satisfy the philanthropist's self-regard. But the violence of his statement too easily lends itself to a reactionary application he can hardly approve.

One could say, perhaps, that Emerson sometimes suffers a loss of wisdom from the other basic danger life involves, an excess of power. It is a danger much more difficult to ascertain in his thought because he is not as concerned with an excess of power as with an excess of form. He seems to feel that there is less danger from it, because there is less likelihood of it. And we must take care to note how he conceives of a problem of too much power. How is it possible to have an excess of spirit, of soul, of moral power, especially when there is usually such a conspicuous absence of it? Emerson never answers this question directly, but he does show a concern for an excess of power in the special sense of the concrete manifestation of power, in the sense that the excess or "acridity" of a virtue amounts to a vice (*W*, VI, 251).

Successful endeavor, for example, depends on a native vitality partly physical, partly mental. Emerson never slights the need for such vitality, insists it cannot be done without, but he also warns that it is often found in a quantity excessive enough to make it a dangerous potential for destructiveness (*W*, VI, 71–72). Such an excess, he feels, is reflected in the reckless, egotistical fury with which Americans pursue business and politics, a fury possibly destructive of all the finer accomplishments of mankind, paid for with suffering and blood, for the sake of personal gain, not deliberately, perhaps, but inadvertently, out of blindness, and culpable just the same (*W*, VII, 289; *W*, XI, 388, 521). Emerson is also concerned that man, with his inventions harnessing the energy and force of nature, is acquiring physical power beyond his moral capacity to use wisely. Anything that frees talent without simultaneously increasing self-command he regards as noxious, and the entire meaning of an excess of power he defines as power unaccompanied by a necessary control (*W*, VII, 166; *W*, X, 20–21).

We also find an excess of power in too strict an application of ideals to daily living. Like it or not, we must pursue all sorts of mundane activities; for this necessary aspect of our lives a fixation on ideal truth would prove a fatal hindrance: had it thus fixed its vision, Emerson remarks, mankind "should have been burned or frozen long ago" (*W*, XI, 536; *W*, III, 237). Not only does an excess of idealism incapacitate a man for daily living, it leads to intolerance and fanaticism. For Thoreau, Emerson claims the effect was an isolation more complete than actually desired, depriving him of the necessary amount of human society for health (*W*, X, 478–79).[11] For more conventional idealists, the reformers, the effect is energy concentrated on some few issues to the point that it becomes merely destructive (*W*, III, 260–61).

Destructiveness, in fact, is the symptom or consequence of an excess of power, and here lies the potential of power to harm and the need for a balance of power and form. But such a balance, especially for a reformer, is extremely delicate. Reinhold Niebuhr is also convinced of the need for balance and aware of the difficulty of attaining it. Social action, he explains, requires the illusion—and it is only an illusion—that men can achieve perfect justice in society, because a "sublime madness" generated by the illusory hope for the perfect is indispensable to achieve any kind of approximation. Only such madness will accept the terrible odds in the struggle for justice. "The illusion [however] is dangerous because it encourages terrible fanaticisms. It must therefore be brought under the control of reason." But so to control it involves the risk of destroying the necessary illusion.[12] A balance as tenuous as this may be flatly impossible, and that is the basic problem of reform. Emerson is aware of it, but does not encourage the fanaticism since he is concerned more with the religious quality of life than with social justice and therefore rests his hope in the individual.

But he also recognizes a need for fanaticism, whether moral or not, in social action and often adopts a tolerant attitude toward it. Disagreeable as each particular reform movement may be, all together, he asserts, they form one movement that is sublime (*W*, I, 270–71). Although perhaps immediately destructive, they are eventually useful, because nature uses everything and turns all malfeasance and evil to good (*W*, VI, 252). Because of this fact, however, we cannot always trace triumphs of civilization to the origins we might wish. Even though he did not like it, Emerson considered trade, the organization of greed, to be the greatest single benefactor of civilization at that time, and he felt that the capitalists building the railroads were performing an involuntary service vastly greater than any intentional philanthropy on record (*W*, VII, 166; *W*, VI, 256). But we must keep in mind that although humanity can be and is benefited in such ways, the agents themselves suffer for it, individuals and particular

[11] For an account of Emerson's and Thoreau's differences that is partial to Thoreau, see Porte's *Emerson and Thoreau*, chaps. 5 and 6; for an account more partial to Emerson, see Leonard Newfeldt's "The Severity of the Ideal: Emerson's 'Thoreau,'" *ESQ*, No. 58 (1970): 77–84.

[12] *Moral Man and Immoral Society* (New York: Scribner's, 1932), p. 277.

societies alike, for nature and destiny are logical, consistent, and virtue, the sentiment of the right, is the eventual and inevitable victor in the universe of Emerson's conception (*J*, IV, 96–97; *W*, XI, 389; *W*, VI, 93–94).

Emerson can tolerate the excess of power as a means to good ends because of his belief in polarity, compensation, according to which power and form, in the long run, automatically maintain a balance. An excess of power or form brings its own antidote:

The longer the drought lasts the more is the atmosphere surcharged with water. The faster the ball falls to the sun, the force to fly off is by so much augmented. And in morals, wild liberty breeds iron conscience; natures with great impulses have great resources, and return from far. In politics, the sons of democrats will be whigs; whilst red republicanism in the father is a spasm of nature to engender an intolerable tyrant in the next age. On the other hand, conservatism, ever more timorous and narrow, disgusts the children and drives them for a mouthful of fresh air into radicalism. (*W*, VI, 64)

Checks to an evil will eventually appear, for the world is always equal to itself, and in nature there is no unemployed force. All decomposition is recomposition, and war disorganizes only to reorganize (*W*, II, 100; *W*, X, 247–48). The balance is strictly and inevitably kept.

Yet once again it is the application of polarity to human affairs that sometimes leads Emerson into a complacency that can be irritating: "In spite of our imbecility and terrors, the 'universal decay of religion,' etc., etc., the moral sense reappears to-day with the same morning newness that has been from of old the fountain of beauty and strength." There is always religion, he continues, and though it may often seem primarily negative, it "will yield spontaneous forms in their due hour" (*W*, VI, 212–13). He may be right (although events up to now fail to prove it), but his tone is too certain, and his certainty is too remote from the problems that faith of any sort faces here and now to be suitable. It should be indicated, however, that at other times Emerson clearly states that he hopes there has been no real loss of religion (*W*, X, 205). He is, after all, concerned about the possible death of God. But the hope of a balance is a slight confession that maybe, in human affairs, power and form do not balance quite so neatly as in nature. Hence Emerson often adopts the more certain tone.

Emerson's theory of the relationship of power and form can lead him, on occasion, into a complacency about the affairs of society, although only when he views them in the broadest context. But with regard to a pet faith of the nineteenth-century—the doctrine of progress—he never lapses into a sentimental reliance on it. At times he declares that there is no progress at all; the law of polarity keeps the balance, so that society recedes as fast and as much on one side as it gains on the other. The proof is the equality among the great men of various ages (*W*, II, 84–86). But in addition to polarity there is the law of evolution; if one is applicable to society, the other should be. And Emerson expresses the belief that among the masses of men (as contrasted to the great men), there is progress (*W*, XI, 147). In other words, the progress does not originate, is not manifested, in the growing superiority of man, but in the moral improvement of more and more men. A society can be superior to another, not in the sense of having better men—goodness is virtue itself, oneness with being, beyond comparative—but in the sense of having more good men so that a more general application of the moral law is facilitated. Social progress, then, rather than being automatic, depends on the individual's personal decision for self-improvement.[13]

The improvement is possible because men are wiser or better than they know (*W*, II, 96). And it is the ideal purpose—the true purpose—of society to educe this innate goodness and wisdom and thereby help form character (*W*, III, 215–16). But this is also a duty of the individual himself, which he finally must do for himself, for the self-formation of character is the only means of attaining personal and social order and is the only defense against the chaos that one often suffers in society (*W*, X, 279–80). Social order must come from the individual, because there can be no order or concert in two people when there is none in one, when the individual is not truly individual, but is divided, alienated from himself. Union, therefore, must be inward, and true or ideal union can only be achieved in an actual individualism (*W*, III, 265–67). In other words, the condition and improvement of society depend, ultimately, on the relationship of power and form in the individual, and that is why Emerson addresses himself primarily, throughout his work, to that relationship.[14] It is both the beginning and the end of his social theory.

[13] Mildred Silver developed this idea in "Emerson and the Idea of Progress," *American Literature* 12 (1940): 18–19.

[14] Two writers take Emerson to task for his refusal to consider politics more seriously and personally: Loren Baritz, *City on a Hill: A History of Ideas and Myths in America* (New York, London, Sydney: Wiley, 1965), pp. 240–60; and John G. Cawelti, *Apostles of the Self-Made Man* (Chicago: University of Chicago Press, 1965), pp. 93–95. They have a point of course, but then, one can add without cynicism, so does Emerson.

Chapter III

The Soul Incarnate
The Power and Form of the Individual

THE INDIVIDUAL BODY is a temporal fixation of atoms, and the mind a temporal arrest of spiritual powers, which in their released state compose the currents of matter and power in the world (*W*, XII, 27–28). In their configurations the atoms and powers are subject to circumstance, physical and mental limitation, all that one cannot do or avoid (*W*, VI, 14–15, 20). As a result it is the universal experience of men that they cannot achieve what they desire, that there always exists a chasm between the promise of ideal power and the shabby experience of its fulfillment (*W*, IV, 184–85). Incomplete in his integrity, unable fully to obey natural law voluntarily, a man is encamped but not domesticated in nature, and his performance never measures up to the promise he feels (*W*, I, 338–39; W, III, 189–90). He is always partial, an approximation of the wholeness one finds in nature, and his accomplishments are consequently partial and approximate (*W*, III, 225, 226–27). His condition of partiality bespeaks the fact that he is a finite creature, a form subject to limitation.

He is, in part, self-limited: it seems to be a condition of incarnation that the private self should tend to prefer private and finite interests over the general law of universal being (*W*, I, 165). His consciousness easily becomes a jail, for having spoken or acted in a certain way, he tends to feel committed to that position, instinctively desiring consistency and working toward it as an end and good in itself (*W*, II, 49, 56). And he normally permits facts and events to tyrannize over his consciousness; he becomes their victim rather than their master (*W*, II, 32–33). These forms of limitation could almost be called self-induced, because they are not totally unavoidable; nevertheless they are the result of an inherent weakness that men find difficult to overcome.

But as a form man is also subject to unavoidable limitations of inheritance. A person's success or lack of it depends considerably on the amount of energy he has inherited, which is highly variable (*W*, VI, 55, 57, 59–61). Moreover, the form inherited—mental as well as physical—sets insuperable limits to one's life: the ditchdigger cannot be an engineer, nor can the engineer be a poet , for their powers are limited by their particular inherited talents. "Every spirit makes its house; but afterwards the house confines the spirit" (*W*, VI, 8–11). The individual also inherits a certain temperament and set of moods, both of which largely control the patterns of his perception, interpretation, and response to his world: his beliefs and unbeliefs are to a great extent structural (*W*, III, 50, 82–83; *W*, IV, 175).

No matter how unpleasant the admission, the fact remains that a man's power is constrained by a many-faceted, general necessity which, as long as he is ignorant and thereby its victim, he calls fate (*W*, VI, 19–20; *W*, X, 73). Even thought is not above fate, for thought too must accord with eternal laws, since anything fantastic in it would contradict our fundamental assumption of the essentially lawful nature of all phenomena. "The limitation is impassable by any insight of man. In its last and loftiest ascensions, insight itself and the freedom of the will, is one of its obedient members" (*W*, VI, 21). In the highest sense, fate is equivalent to the basic law of cause and effect, which is inescapable, but nevertheless is not incompatible with—in fact, as we have seen, it is necessary for—freedom. Emerson gives fate its due, then affirms that man is nevertheless and therefore free.

In his interpretation, there are two basic aspects of nature: on the one hand, fate, natural laws, the order of things, necessity; on the other, will, duty, or freedom, creative forces that stem from thought or consciousness (*W*, XI, 231; *W*, VI, 25). He frankly confesses that he cannot logically reconcile these two aspects, and he resorts to an old and honorable Christian paradox: "To hazard the contradiction,— freedom is necessary. If you please to plant yourself on the side of Fate, and say, Fate is all; then we say, a part of Fate is the freedom of man" (*W*, VI, 23). Perceiving fate, or necessity, a man must choose whether he will within himself obey it or not: that is, he is not free not to choose. But beyond that, as a consequence of the proper choice, he acquires freedom in a different sense: it consists paradoxically in "a voluntary obedience, a necessitated freedom," that is, a willing submission to fate, or necessity, the basic law of God's order, which, when properly understood, is no longer fate but Providence, by which he can attain what he wills (*W*, VI, 240). Emerson bases his faith in our freedom upon experience: "Forever wells up the impulse of choosing and acting in the soul" (*W*, VI, 23).[1]

[1] Compare Whitman's statement on the same problem: "The whole Universe is absolute Law. Freedom only opens entire activity and license *under the law*. To the degraded or undevelopt—and even to too many others—the thought of freedom is a thought of escaping from law—which, of course, is impossible.... While we are from birth to death the subjects of irresistible law, enclosing every movement and minute, we yet escape, by a paradox, into true

He is willing to place his faith in his experience of freedom because he is aware that in the study of phenomena from a strictly causational premise—from a scientific point of view alone—there is no escape from the links of the chain of physical and metaphysical necessity (*W*, III, 54), as Jonathan Edwards's powerful argument demonstrates. That is why, after describing the nature and extent of necessity, Emerson says that we should not continually enlarge the generalization of fate but "seek to do justice to the other elements as well," that is, should consider phenomena from other points of view (*W*, VI, 21). As Hugo Münsterberg has noted, Emerson can say that intellect annuls fate because the very construction of a theory of necessity bespeaks the will's freedom to observe phenomena from a causal point of view, to choose its angle of vision.[2] Fate is just one more idea of the intellect, as Emerson's opening paragraph of "Fate" shows. Thus intellect is a creative power which, if we are honest with our own experience, cannot be ignored or denied (*W*, III, 54). Because the world is plastic and fluid to God, it is the same to those of His attributes that we share and exercise (*W*, I, 105), and intellect is one of those attributes. A man is "a lonely thought harmoniously organized into correspondence with the universe of mind and matter" (*W*, X, 200), and his power stems from both aspects of this description, his intellect, and his corresponding relation to the universe. Intellect is the basic, simple power anterior to all action and construction, apprising men of spiritual facts—rights, duties, thoughts—which are aspects of one essence, truth (*W*, II, 325; *W*, XII, 37–38). The more intellect the more power; for thought affirms a necessity of design in nature that cannot be separated from thought and will but must always have coexisted with them. Upon perceiving nature's design and voluntarily submitting to it, we are no longer ruled by it but preside over it by willing what must be. "All power is of one kind, a sharing of the nature of the world," and we share it through our correspondence with it and through understanding that correspondence (*W*, VI, 27–28, 56). Will is inseparable from intellect and from

---

free will. Strange as it may seem, we only attain to freedom by a knowledge of, and implicit obedience to, Law.... For there is to the highest, that law as absolute as any—more absolute than any—the Law of Liberty." "Freedom," in *Prose Works 1892*, ed. Floyd Stovall, 2 (New York: New York University Press, 1964): 537–38.

[2] "Emerson as Philosopher," in *Harvard Psychological Studies*, 2 (1906): 28. One can call Emerson's insight into the problem basically existential, as Paul Roubiczek's analysis of the existential premise shows: "As the [scientific] method is designed to disclose necessity, freedom can never be proved in this way; to discover it we must start from experience." *Existentialism: For and Against* (Cambridge: Cambridge University Press, 1964), p. 14.

the design perceived by the intellect; for perceiving it, we must either accept it or reject it, move toward it or away from it. Will does not mean willfulness, for willfulness is only one direction of the will—away from the design—and signifies weakness, a failure to share in the nature of the world (*W*, I, 39–40; *W*, X, 91–92). But we can make the design our own—and thus make its power, which is the only power, our own—only through intellect and will, which are complementary aspects of our spiritual being. And design makes sense only as an aspect of our spiritual being: without conscious perception and formulation it in effect does not exist.

The intellect itself can be divided into two categories. Each of us possesses certain aptitudes peculiar to himself, but in addition he has, in common with other men, a higher, visionary faculty, the attributes of which are self-existence, eternity, intuition, and command. It is the mind behind all minds that constitutes us as men, so that it is more proper to say that we belong to it than to say that it belongs to us (*W*, X, 93). These categories, or faculties, the conception of which he found in Coleridge, Emerson often calls the understanding and the reason, respectively: "Reason is the highest faculty of the soul—what we mean often by the soul itself; it never *reasons*, never proves, it simply perceives; it is vision. The Understanding toils all the time, compares, contrives, adds, argues, near-sighted but strong-sighted, dwelling in the present the expedient the customary. Beasts have some understanding but no Reason. Reason is potentially perfect in every man—Understanding in very different degrees of strength."[3] The understanding deals with phenomena in space and time exclusively, while the reason, although not alien to the realm of phenomenal existence, perceives in addition supersensible ideas, such as right and wrong, or the law of cause and effect, or the correspondence of the laws of matter and mind (*W*, I, 36). These two modes of intellect can also be called materialistic and idealistic, the former founded in the experience of the senses, the latter founded on consciousness, on thought and will. Both modes of thinking are natural, but one is higher than and inclusive of the other. The understanding depends on the senses, and the senses, Emerson says, "give us representations of things but what are the things themselves, they cannot tell." The reason, on the contrary, discovers or reveals facts that do not depend on the senses, for the facts and it are of the same nature (*W*, I, 329–30). Through the one we gain physical dominion: technology; through the other, spiritual dominion, or truth: geometry.

The understanding is a faculty that man as a finite being possesses

[3] *The Letters of Ralph Waldo Emerson*, ed. Ralph L. Rusk, 1 (New York: Columbia University Press, 1939): 412–13.

and can use according to his capacity; it is the translation of pure spirit into power on an inferior plane of existence, the human equivalent of *natura naturans*. Space and time, society, labor, climate, and food, locomotion, organic and mechanical forces, all properties of matter, are the subjects of its exercise, and with these subjects it adds, divides, combines, and measures, discerns difference, likeness, and order, and applies manifold forces to particular ends (*W*, I, 36–37). The cast of mind resulting from the use of the understanding is prudential; it learns the laws of material nature, not to go behind nature and explore or contemplate its origin, beauty, or value, but to keep its laws and use them for material benefit. It is the virtue of the senses, the outmost action of the inward life, "God taking thought for oxen" (*W*, II, 224–25, 222). And prudence is a virtue, because it is necessary for survival (*W*, VIII, 3).

To live, however, by the understanding alone has undesirable effects. Men are prone to apply it to areas beyond its sphere; because of some errors or absurdities it discovers, say, in a church or in an object of veneration, it finds error in the very sentiment of worship (*W*, X, 220–21). Generally it tends to suppress the imagination and leads to a "priapism of the senses and the understanding," which results in a cheap materialism, life on the same plane with ants and bees (*W*, V, 255, 83). Such a materialism—concerned only with material means to material ends—is a disease, a figurative "thickening of the skin until the vital organs are destroyed" (*W*, II, 223). It is a disease because it severs the pleasure of the senses from the needs of character, severs sensual gratification from morality, living from virtue (*W*, II, 103–4).[4]

The point is that man's power alone confines man, limits his total power so that the desirable balance between power and form is upset. For that reason Emerson considers limitation the essential sin (*W*, VII, 295; *W*, II, 308). It is necessary not to ignore, suppress, or deny the function of the understanding, but to use it in its proper role: "The world of the senses is a world of shows; it does not exist for itself, but has a symbolic character; and a true prudence or law of shows recognizes the co-presence of other laws and knows that its own office is subaltern; knows that it is surface and not centre where it works. Prudence is false when detached. It is legitimate when it is

<hr/>

[4] Robert C. Pollock contends that to Emerson the essential problem of his contemporaries was that "they had accepted the fiction of a split universe, that is, a universe in which the life of the spirit is insulated from man's life in nature." "Ralph Waldo Emerson, 1803–1882: The Single Vision" in *American Classics Reconsidered: A Christian Appraisal*, ed. Harold C. Gardiner, S.J. (New York: Scribner's, 1958), p. 18.

the Natural History of the soul incarnate, when it unfolds the beauty of laws within the narrow scope of the senses" (*W*, II, 222). The higher intellect, reason, frees us from the despotism of our senses, introduces us to the realm of the supersensible, of causes, ideas, morality, and thereby raises us from the particular to the universal, from forms alone to power and form. And it is by virtue of our conscious participation in universal power that we become men, as distinguished from animals (*W*, I, 49–50; *W*, X, 185). The materialistic mode of thought is necessary, but must, for the sake of the whole man, be subordinated to the reason.

Of all organisms, only man is an entrance to the unfathomed sea of thought and virtue (*W*, I, 45–46). Although we live in succession, division, and parts, within us is the whole, the eternal one, the reason— and it is not to be distinguished from the divine essence (*W*, II, 269). This conception of the soul is Plotinian rather than orthodox Christian, the Christian having held that God is a part of the soul, a spark or breath or voice in it, particularly the soul in a state of grace.[5] But Emerson, it should be emphasized, never intends his conception to be used as a basis for egoism. To call the reason ours, or even human, is to him an impertinence (*J*, III, 235); it is the universal soul, the Over-Soul, and while it works within man's individual life, we are essentially contained in it and related to one another through it (*W*, II, 268; *W*, I, 27). Although he naturalizes the operation of Christian grace, Emerson, as Theodore Parker stressed, never confuses man with God. Man is the effect, God the cause.[6]

But, because of its nature, there is in the soul itself no bar or wall between the cause and the effect. "We lie open on one side to the deeps of spiritual nature, to the attributes of God" (*W*, II, 270–71). Because the reason is the whole within man, its perceptions abolish or transcend the limits of time and space, which for the understanding prove insurmountable (*W*, II, 272–73). The higher intellect separates its perceptions from all local and personal considerations, sees the principles behind the particular forms, beholds identity and eternal causation, the self-existence of truth and right, with the result that duration and extent are no longer all-significant (*W*, II, 325– 26, 69). In thus stripping time of its illusions, we come to see that it

---

[5] See Kenneth W. Cameron, *Emerson the Essayist*, 1 (Raleigh, N.C.: The Thistle Press, 1945): 53; Brother F. Joseph Paulits, *Emerson's Concept of Good and Evil* (Ph.D. dissertation, University of Pittsburgh, 1954), pp. 51–52; and Stephen E. Whicher, *Freedom and Fate: An Inner Life of Ralph Waldo Emerson* (Philadelphia, University of Pennsylvania Press, 1953), p. 21.

[6] Parker said that Emerson "never sinks God in man." "The Writings of Ralph Waldo Emerson," in *Parker*, 10: 228.

is not duration, but the quality or depth of the moment that is truly important. "We pierce to the eternity, of which time is a flitting surface"; a slight revelation, a slight increase of power of thought, makes life seem to be of vast duration, which we call time, but a more profound insight makes us realize an order that is other and higher than time (*W*, VII, 183).

And yet it is not quite right to imply that we actively attain this revelation. Rather, we obey the impulses of the soul, receive the truth of the Over-Soul and become organs of its power. "When we discern justice, when we discern truth, we do nothing of ourselves, but allow a passage to its beams" (*W*, II, 270–71, 63–64). This influx is revelation, the introduction of the infinite into the finite.

Paul Tillich's analysis of the relation between the temporal and eternal can help us understand what Emerson means:

> If it is our destiny to participate in freedom in the divine life here and now, in and above time, we can say that the "evil one" is he from whom we pray to be delivered: It is the enslaving power which prevents us from fulfilling our human destiny; it is the wall that separates us from the eternal life to which we belong; and it is the sickness of our being and that of our world caused by this separation. Salvation happens whenever the enslaving power is conquered, whenever the wall is broken through, whenever the sickness is healed. He who can do this is called the saviour. Nobody except God can do this. . . . All liberating, all healing power comes from the other side of the wall which separates us from eternal life. Whenever it appears, it is a manifestation of eternal, divine life in our temporal and motal existence.[7]

The "evil one," as Tillich describes it, is equivalent to what Emerson calls limitation, the essential sin. As we have seen, Emerson contends that the individual himself erects this wall between himself and his cause—as a result of consciousness and the discovery of will—and that he himself can remove it by relinquishing his will (paradoxically, an act of will), by opening himself to God. Then can come what he variously describes as the realization of his own powers—the God within—or, more often, as an influx of the Over-Soul—the entrance of God's attributes. To Emerson it amounts to the same thing: he distinguishes without separating cause and effect. The point is not that

---

[7] *The Eternal Now* (New York: Scribner's, 1963), p. 115. For a good discussion of the similarities between Emerson and Tillich, see Paul Lauter's "Emerson Through Tillich," *ESQ*, No. 31 (1963): 49–55. Hyatt Waggoner has pointed out the close resemblance of Emerson's depiction of the influx of divinity to Edwards's concept of grace: " 'Grace' in the Thought of Emerson, Thoreau, and Hawthorne," *ESQ*, No. 54 (1969): 68–69. (Waggoner is aware, of course, of the crucial differences.)

Emerson's and Tillich's theological positions are identical—they are not—but that both men describe the same experience, as the similarity of their analyses indicates, and draw similar conclusions from it.

The soul is not an organ or a faculty but the power potentially animating our organs and faculties; it is not the intellect or will but the proper master of the intellect and will. By acting in it the intellect becomes genius, the will virtue, the affection love (*W*, II, 270–71). And by submitting to it we come to live in thoughts and act with energies of immortal power (*W*, II, 296).[8]

Later in his career Emerson tended to call this power, in its human manifestation, instinct, and he described it in mythic terms as "a shapeless giant in the cave, massive, without hands or fingers or articulating lips or teeth or tongue; Behemoth, disdaining speech, disdaining particulars, lurking, surly, invincible, disdaining thoughts, always whole, never distributed, aboriginal, old as Nature." But he allied it just as directly with the power of God as he previously had related the reason (*W*, XII, 35). Whicher remarked that this indicated a shift in Emerson's thinking from a belief in the spirituality of power, the effect in men of divine inspiration, to a belief that the creative power of men and God was more closely related to the amoral aboriginal physical force in nature.[9] However, Emerson also termed this power instinct rather early in his career (*W*, II, 64). In interpreting his use of the term, we must recall his conception of the ascending metamorphosis of power from one plane of existence to another. We should also remember Emerson's knack for observing the evolutionary scale from a historical or an idealistic point of view. In historical, human terms, instinct is the aboriginal power which, when metamorphosed in the mind, ascends to suggestions that in expression become intellectual and moral laws (*W*, XII, 59–60, 68). It is in mankind that the power and laws in nature acquire their moral and spiritual significance—or, rather, that their moral and spiritual significance are realized. To Emerson, this metamorphosis can be paradoxically regarded as both divine inspiration and as historical evolution, without contradiction.

The reason, then, is the power, superior to the understanding, which intuitively perceives ideas. Emerson accepts Plato's definition of ideas as simple, permanent, uniform, and self-existent; and he further contends that they are the mental equivalents of the laws that determine all phenomena, and that they can only be intuited (*W*, IV, 85–86; *W*,

[8] See Jonathan Bishop, *Emerson on the Soul*, especially pp. 19–25, for a brilliant explanation of the soul as Emerson conceived it.

[9] *Freedom and Fate*, p. 149.

I, 55; *W*, II, 64).[10] The facts or ideas perceived by the reason have an innate superiority over the reports of the understanding because they are unaffected by the illusions of the senses. The ideas intuited can be relied upon because they are of the same nature as the reason itself, so that in the reason's perception "the act of seeing and the thing seen, the seer and the spectacle, the subject and the object, are one" (*W*, I, 330; *W*, II, 269). The ideas do not contradict the order of material phenomena, but contain it, because the reason and material phenomena share a common origin (*W*, II, 64). This origin is also the origin of the one mind common to all of us that makes it possible for us to share a common world of thought and feeling, to communicate and to understand each other's perceptions (*W*, II, 3). The very fact that we intuit ideas, that we apply them, and that we share them, satisfies Emerson that matter and mind have a common transcendent origin.[11]

Finally, when the higher intellect perceives an idea, a facet of truth, there arises the desire to enact it; this desire along with the perception is the moral sentiment, an integrated aspect of the reason and the ultimate source of creative power (*W*, VI, 28; *W*, I, 272). By means of the moral sentiment we can envision the grandeur of justice, the eternity of moral nature, and the victory of love, especially love, which is the redeemer and instructor, as it is the primal essence, of the soul (*W*, X, 83; *W*, VI, 218). Many of our problems stem from our tendency to separate wisdom from holiness, intellect from moral nature, whereas our spiritual health and power require their integration (*W*, VIII, 228; *W*, I, 221; *W*, VIII, 317: *W*, XII, 60–61). Emerson believes it insufficient to see evils without being moved to enact their remedy, and the first step to their remedy is to strive for virtue, which we do by taking the direction of the moral sentiment rather than that of the private self (*W*, III, 102; *W*, X, 83). We should will without being willful.

[10] In the heyday of nineteenth-century science, intuition, of course, was discounted as a valid means of intellectual inquiry. C. S. Peirce was one of the first to reinvoke the value of intuition by asserting that induction and deduction can only test ideas, and that the ideas themselves must originate in "abduction," or intuition. See Frederic I. Carpenter, "William James and Emerson," *American Literature* 9 (1939):55.

[11] Compare Whitehead's remarks on the latter point: "I do not understand how a common world of thought can be established in the absence of a common world of sense. I will not argue this point in detail; but in the absence of a transcendence of thought, or a transcendence of the world of sense, it is difficult to see how the subjectivist is to divest himself of his solitariness." *Science and the Modern World*, p. 131.

Our power rests in intellect and will, the exercise of which is self-reliance. On the level of the understanding, in terms of succeeding according to ordinary values, self-reliance means the fulfillment of one's particular talents and aptitudes, one's specialty or bias (*W*, VIII, 306–7). For practical success, a certain amount of physical passion and force, which varies from person to person, is necessary (*J*, IV, 96; *W*, VI, 259). To a certain degree, egotism is also necessary, the success of the English being for Emerson a striking example (*J*, IX, 519; *W*, V, 148).

But without the higher intellect and the moral sentiment, self-reliance is for Emerson finally spurious, not actually power but simply so much futile "horsepower" (*W*, X, 96). Individualism requires the guidance of the universal mind to give it a moral direction; without that direction it will finally defeat itself, for virtue and right are always victorious (*W*, XII, 50; *J*, IV, 97). While passion is necessary as a spring of action, it must be transformed into a better nature, just as following one's bias should involve the reason and the moral sentiment (*W*, VI, 259; *W*, VIII, 306–7, 307–8). But the determination of a proper, as opposed to an improper, self-reliance is very difficult:

I know it is a nice point to discriminate this self-trust, which is the pledge of all mental vigor and performance, from the disease to which it is allied,—the exaggeration of the part which we can play;—yet they are two things. But it is sanity to know that, over my talent or knack, and a million times better than any talent, is the central intelligence which subordinates and uses all talents; and it is only as a door into this, that any talent or the knowledge it gives is of value. He only who comes into this central intelligence, in which no egotism or exaggeration can be, comes into self-possession. (*W*, VII, 295)

Although the discrimination is not easy, Emerson feels that perfect candor with oneself makes it possible. And it must be made for genuine self-reliance and self-fulfillment: its difficulty serves as no argument against its necessity.

The self-reliance Emerson explains and advocates is based on his belief that the whole is in each man and is the source of worth of each man (*W*, II, 5). Self-reliance is Emerson's interpretation of the sentences of Luke—"The kingdom of God is within you"—and Paul—"We are the temple of the living God." [12] He emphasizes throughout his career that the reliance should be placed in that which is the cause; that as an effect a man should never lose sight of the truth that he did not create himself; that he is a manifestation of powers not his own;

[12] As Mildred Silver indicates in "Emerson and the Idea of Progress," p. 11.

and that he therefore should never transfer his reliance to himself as an effect (*W*, X, 206; see also, e.g., *W*, II, 69–70, and *W*, I, 122).[13] Such a transfer is the fall, the disease of the will, rebellion and separation from the eternal to which he feels every man properly belongs (*W*, II, 105–6).

Self-reliance means obedience to that which is larger than ourselves, the cause, for in ourselves we are ephemeral. Egotism is ultimately, in terms of the necessity in nature, the mark of weakness; man must have something above himself to venerate, for without it he is impoverished, having only himself (*W*, I, 391; *W*, X, 206). Worship and reliance should be placed in power, not in forms,[14] but obedience to power requires courage—which Emerson defines as being equal to the problems facing us—to save us from the perilous edge of destruction on which we are standing (*W*, IV, 236–37; *W*, VII, 264). Life requires courage, and self-reliance as a response to life requires courage, because it means dealing absolutely in the world, as if one were entirely alone, with the conviction that should all perish one can, with God, make all anew. Self-reliance demands that a man have the courage to be, in large part, isolated from his fellow men, he alone with God alone (*W*, II, 309; *W*, X, 83; *W*, VI, 322, 325).

Self-reliance requires courage, but, to make it even more difficult, it is a duty. The fact that a man's soul is God-within places on him a tremendous responsibility to it and even for it.[15] Moreover, all real good or harm that can befall a man can come only from himself; he is responsible for his own condition (*J*, III, 200; *W*, I, 122; *W*, VI, 39–40). Hence it is his duty to submit to the moral sentiment, the essence of which is "ought," to do the duty of the moment and abstain from doing the wrong, and he especially ought because the

---

[13] *Early Lectures*, 2: 247–48; *Young Emerson Speaks: Unpublished Discourses on Many Subjects*, ed. Arthur C. McGiffert (Boston: Houghton Mifflin, 1938), p. 238. Harry Hayden Clark thoroughly documents his assertion that Emerson consistently emphasized "his doctrine of immutable laws and of the need for disciplining one's self to obey them." "Conservative and Mediatory Emphases in Emerson's Thought," in *Transcendentalism and Its Legacy*, pp. 30–32. Pollock points out that Emerson's doctrine of self-reliance inevitably, given his background and immediate culture, had a "bourgeois tinge," but that this should not be confused with the doctrine's essential meaning: "The Single Vision," p. 41.

[14] Hence Emerson, although believing Christ to be a realization of the potential divinity of man, rejects the implications of this belief, indicated by F. O. Matthiessen, that there is nothing more important than the individual and that man does not find his completion in something greater than himself. See *American Renaissance: Art and Expression in the Age of Emerson and Whitman* (New York: Oxford University Press, 1941), p. 446.

[15] *Young Emerson Speaks*, pp. 105–6.

moral sentiment is the voice of God Himself (*W*, I, 120–21; *W*, X, 225). Most men are frightened by it because it is the voice of God and bespeaks His pervasive, governing, simple, terrible laws; they would prefer to use intermediaries, to evade, but in Emerson's view, for that very reason, one should enter into a direct relation with one's creator (*W*, X, 96–97; *W*, VI, 214). "With every influx of light comes new danger. Has he light? He must bear witness to the light, and always outrun that sympathy which gives him such keen satisfaction, by his fidelity to new revelations of the incessant soul" (*W*, II, 99). Self-reliance, therefore, is arduous; it requires self-knowledge and the courage to enact that knowledge. "If any one imagines that this law is lax, let him keep its commandment one day" (*W*, II, 74). It cannot be perfectly kept, but the law requires that one try because one's soul is at stake.

It also requires that one try every day, because the soul is incessant: "man was made for conflict, not for rest." Becoming civilized, in a high sense, means ceasing from fixed ideas (the truest state of mind rested in becomes false) and learning the secret of cumulative power. "Life only avails, not the having lived. Power ceases in the instant of repose; it resides in the moment of transition from a past to a new state, in the shooting of the gulf, in the darting to an aim." It is in transition—the rise of a thought from the unconscious to the conscious, and the enactment of the thought—not in goals themselves that a man acquires power, for the soul, in this world of parts, becomes. To speak of self-reliance is actually a poor external mode of explanation; we should speak, Emerson says, of that which relies, because it works and is (*W*, XII, 60; *W*, I, 94–95; *W*, VII, 20; *W*, II, 69–70).

Emerson poses the paradox that within each man is the whole, being itself, but because he is finite and lives in a world of phenomenal existence, he must realize being through a process of becoming. He must grow, just as organisms grow and all of nature grows, through the process of evolution, just as God is being yet incessantly creates in each moment. And the key to a man's growth is thought, for his whole life, whether consciously or not, is the outcome of his thought (*W*, II, 161):

The life of man is a self-evolving circle, which, from a ring imperceptibly small, rushes on all sides outwards to new and larger circles, and that without end. The extent to which this generation of circles, wheel without wheel, will go, depends on the force or truth of the individual soul. For it is the inert effort of each thought, having formed itself into a circular wave of circumstance,—as, for instance, an empire, rules of an art, a local usage, a religious rite,—to heap itself on that ridge, and to solidify and hem in the life. But if the soul is quick and strong, it bursts over that boundary on all sides and expands another orbit on the great deep, which also runs up into a high wave, with attempt again to stop and to bind. But the heart refuses to be imprisoned; in its first and narrowest pulses, it already tends outward with a vast force and to immense and innumerable expansions. (*W*, II, 304)

He must continue growing because he is always in a crisis, always on the brink of chaos, always in danger of suffering calamity. In order to survive, to live deeply and truly, he must expand into a new thought, for each new step in thought reconciles what before were discordant facts, and with reconciliation comes understanding and mastery of them, or power (*W*, II, 124, 308; *W*, VII, 163–64; *W*, XII, 380). "A new perception, the smallest new activity given to the perceptive power, is a victory won to the living universe from Chaos and old Night," but only so long as the growth resulting from the perception, and the thought attendant upon the perception, are of a certain total character, involving the whole man, because "*so to be* is the sole inlet of *so to know*" (*W*, XII, 402; *W*, II, 320). He must give himself up to being in order to become, and he must continuously become because any being he attains is, in itself, incomplete. Becoming is an aspect of the phenomenal world, the world of parts; and an important part—an indispensable part—of the process of becoming is the casting of thought into a circular wave of circumstance, that is, the conscious creation of forms.

Chapter IV

The Creator in the Finite
The Power and Form of Consciousness

POWER AS SUCH, or the influx of power into man, Emerson calls the intellect receptive. But there is another aspect of man's power, which is the intellect constructive, the mind's generation of forms through the marriage of thought to nature. Thought is spontaneous, or intuitive, but its expression is deliberate, implying a mixture of will, a strenuous exercise of choice (*W*, II, 334, 336). The intellect receptive tends to unity, while the intellect constructive tends to diversity; these are tendencies of the mind and of nature, respectively. "The unity absorbs, and melts or reduces. Nature opens and creates." These two principles, however, rather than contradicting each other, interpenetrate all thought, for in the action of the mind perception melts into will, knowledge into act, or, to reverse the terms, the perceptions of the soul hasten to incarnate themselves in action, to take body (*W*, IV, 51; *W*, II, 325; *W*, XII, 18). In its higher stages the mind, because of its access to the mind of God, is the creator in the finite, its power being a continuation of the power that made it (*W*, I, 64; *W*, XII, 17).

The publication or incarnation of power into forms is essential for health: in accordance with polarity, inlet must be matched by outlet, reception by expression; an imbalance of the two is, accordingly, disease (*W*, X, 76; *W*, III, 5). Hence Emerson describes the man of health as an organizer of facts according to his classification of them, his power varying according to both the depth of his insight and the extent of his ability to translate his insight into some form, into some art, or trade, or science, or mode of living (*W*, VIII, 137; *W*, X, 77; *W*, I, 206).

Some minds tend to be cognizant of resemblance, of identity, and they have traditionally inclined toward philosophy and the arts; while other minds, which concern us now, tend to perceive difference, and they have traditionally belonged to practical men of action, and the creators of material forms (*W*, V, 238; *W*, IV, 150). Such men apply their minds to natural phenomena and organize the forces and resistances therein to the end of producing material goods and wealth (*W*, VI, 85–86; *W*, V, 80–81). But usually they apply their understanding alone—only part of their total power—so that for them the creation of material forms often becomes the sole end (*W*, I, 72).

The consequences are manifold. The man tends a machine, or a trade, or a profession, and insofar as that becomes the end in and of itself, he finds himself metamorphosed into a thing, a victim of his work, a mechanical functionary—that is, he becomes alienated from himself (*W*, I, 83–84; *W*, II, 142; *W*, VI, 285–86). Or, should he acquire some power of physical force or wealth, he desires the more subtle power of politics and business for private ends, and in his quest for it falls into "an easy self-reliance that makes him self-willed and unscrupulous" (*W*, XI, 522). But as all men are responsible for their own condition, and are endowed with a moral awareness of that responsibility, they cannot legitimately transfer the guilt for their misdeeds to the customary practices of their trade or profession. The unscrupulous creator of material wealth must pay the compensatory price of self-alienation: an eventual loss of faith and content and an immersion in a profound melancholy (*W*, II, 140; *W*, VIII, 331).

Creating material goods and wealth for personal power actually represents a perversion of the innate desire for power of a finer kind. Such power, genuine power, effects intellectual and moral perceptions. The perversion results in the loss of genuine power, and the realization of this loss causes the eventual loss of faith and attendant melancholy (*J*, VIII, 219; *W*, VIII, 269; *W*, X, 84–85).[1] As Emerson sees it, western cultures need to correct the nominal theory of success by showing men the other powers they can invoke and the rank of powers they can appeal to (*W*, VI, 131; *W*, I, 107). The need is for growth, the metamorphosis of power, not so that men will cease creating material forms, but so that they will create them as a means of self-expression and self-fulfillment, so that the expenditure of wealth can become united with character, and a man's business can serve both as a means of acquiring and enacting wisdom and virtue (*W*, VII, 109; *W*, X, 129).

Emerson does not disparage the creation of material wealth as such, but he feels that other types of creation—the creation by the higher intellect and moral sentiment of laws, institutions, art, and letters—are superior (*W*, VIII, 302). The perception necessary for such

---

[1] C. G. Jung remarked that a great many of his patients were middle-aged, conventionally successful people who had come to feel that their lives had been and were totally meaningless. "We wholly overlook," Jung said, "the essential fact that the achievements which society rewards are won at the cost of a diminution of personality." He meant personality in a deep sense, of course, and he therefore felt that these patients' problem was essentially religious. See *Modern Man in Search of a Soul* (New York: Harcourt, Brace, 1933), pp. 70, 119–20, 267–68.

creation works by a law of undulation—one must make great efforts at mental concentration, and then forbear activity to see what the Over-Soul will show, or, in other words, allow the idea to emerge from the unconscious to the conscious. To embody an idea in a form one must vigilantly bring the whole intellect to bear on a problem at every moment (*W*, II, 331–32, 340). We could say that such vigilance is necessary for any kind of creation, but it has special significance for the kind we are now discussing. It is not difficult to understand the process by which the understanding creates, because material phenomena and materialistic values are its natural habitat, so to speak, its very tools and objects. But the higher intellect deals with a supersensible reality, so that its embodiment in forms—even social and intellectual forms—presents theoretical problems of which Emerson is well aware.

One problem is the unreliability and inconsecutiveness of inspiration, of the type of insight or thought characteristic of the reason. Such insights cannot be controlled, and the periods between them, the high points of significance in a man's life, are periods of darkness, threatening to destroy his identity (*W*, VIII, 272–73). But the memory serves to transcend this problem, for it is the matrix in which his other faculties are imbedded, the thread preserving and holding together the periods of insight, keeping life and thought from becoming an unrelated succession, and thereby preserving his identity, which is necessary for moral and intellectual action (*W*, XII, 90).

A more serious problem concerns the relation, or lack thereof, between the understanding and the reason. Emerson calls this relationship the double consciousness, because the two show little apparent relation to each other: "one prevails now, all buzz and din; and the other prevails then, all infinitude and paradise; and, with the progress of life, the two discover no greater disposition to reconcile themselves" (*W*, I, 353–54; see also *W*, IV, 178–79). The reason reveals absolute law and answers to the soul's, not the understanding's, questions (*W*, II, 282). Emerson describes it another way: each man has two pairs of eyes, and when the pair above is closed, the pair beneath should be open, and vice versa, but the pair above, representing, of course, the reason, is more important because in its perceptions the facts seen by the lower are given an order and coherence that accord with the great laws of the world (*W*, X, 238). Although as we have seen he occasionally doubts, Emerson generally believes that the intuitive principle of the reason contains within it the logical principle of the understanding, that the two are superficially contradictory but ultimately reconcilable (*W*, II, 329). Hence he urges patience, and still more patience, as well as faith "that this petty web we weave will at last be overshot and reticulated with veins of the blue," that our mundane world will be ennobled by the activity of the soul (*W*, I, 354).[2]

Another problem concerning the higher intellect's creation of forms, which Emerson feels to be new and peculiar to his age, is the mind's awareness of itself (*W*, X, 325): "The ancients were self-united. We have found out the difference of outer and inner. They described. We reason. They acted. We philosophise. They describe what happened. We what is thought and felt."[3] This self-awareness Emerson calls subjectiveness, the withdrawal of attention from the object and the concentration on the subject, and he welcomes it, while denouncing the intellectual egotism with which it is sometimes confused (*W*, XII, 313–14). But he recognizes the danger in it, for he considers it the psychological equivalent of the theological doctrine of the Fall, and perceives that the consequence can be a paralyzing distrust of our own ability to perceive accurately and act wisely (*W*, III, 75–76). This new awareness can also divide a man, cause the very double consciousness, the separation of body and soul, which frustrates the need to act and create. It can produce severance, dissociation, detachment (*W*, X, 326), Emerson's words for self-alienation.[4]

Such detachment poses the problem of alienation from nature. It means that one is constantly aware of the discrepancy between the world one experiences and the world one conceives, aware of the apparent fact that these two worlds run in parallel lines that never meet (*W*, III, 84; *J*, IV, 440–41). Detachment also involves seeing an object in a nonpersonal, universal light which, although perhaps accurate, can cause a discontinuity between the mind and the object, thereby paralyzing the will and thus reducing one's creative power (*W*, XII, 38–39, 44).

But Emerson remains unconvinced that the discontinuity is neces-

[2] Hence Howard Mumford Jones says that Emerson failed convincingly to reconcile man's double nature, his participation in time and eternity. *Belief and Disbelief in American Literature* (Chicago and London: University of Chicago Press, 1967), pp. 66–68. That is to say, as Emerson himself would have agreed, faith is no demonstration.

[3] *Early Lectures*, 2: 168.

[4] This divided condition is, according to Jung, the basis of neurosis. *Modern Man in Search of a Soul*, p. 273. Two critics have pointed out how Emerson anticipated much modern psychological thought: James E. Miller, Jr., "Uncharted Interiors: The American Romantics Revisited," *ESQ*, No. 35 (1964): 35–36; and William E. Bridges, "Transcendentalism and Psychotherapy: Another Look at Emerson," *American Literature* 45 (1969): 157–77.

sary. He points out that Plato, while acknowledging that super-essential being exceeds the limits of the intellect, declares that nevertheless things are knowable because of the correspondence of heaven and earth, matter and mind, part and whole (*W*, IV, 61–62). Sherman Paul, in a brilliant analysis of this problem,[5] has demonstrated how, for Emerson, perception, in the fullest sense of the word, bridges the epistemological gap opened by Descartes between the inner and outer, subject and object, and unifies them in the individual. For although intellect disjoins, affection unites, and in the perception of the total soul—which includes the affections and the moral sentiment—Emerson contends that "the power to see is not separated from the will to do, but the insight proceeds from obedience, and the obedience proceeds from a joyful perception" (*W*, XII, 44; *W*, II, 281). We cannot analyze this total act into a simple sequence: the moral sentiment never stops with insight alone, but fuses insight and affection into will; and the will, in this complex of interrelationships, acts by surrendering to the moral sentiment and intellectual truth. Further, the will surrenders out of the love stimulated by insight, while love serves to stimulate the same perception and insight. To repeat a phrase, "*so to be* is the sole inlet of *so to know*" (*W*, X, 103; *W*, VI, 29–30; *W*, VIII, 229–30, 228; *W*, VII, 309; *W*, II, 320). This complex of factors that overcomes the detachment of subject and object and thereby makes creation possible is what Paul has in mind when he remarks that "the apprehension of unity, represented by the moral sentiment in Emerson's thought, fused subject and object with a religious warmth, and by uniting man with God, sanctified perception as a moral duty."[6]

Emerson sees that intellect alone can divorce power and form, but he contends that it does not have to, that man can enact the pattern of nature: "All forces are found in Nature united with that which they move: heat is not separate, light is not massed aloof, nor electricity, nor gravity, but they are always in combination. And so moral powers; they are thirsts for action, and the more you accumulate, the more they mould and form" (*W*, X, 186). But Emerson insists that external, manipular efforts will not realize the world of thought in forms (*W*, III, 84–85). Living in a subjective age, he feels it necessary to insist that creation, the transformation of power into form, be from within outward (*W*, I, 217–18; *W*, XII, 12), a position consistent, of course, with his organicism.

Emerson constantly emphasizes the need for creation; to him, a thought exists to be expressed, and until it is expressed—embodied

---

[5] See *Emerson's Angle of Vision*, pp. 35–36.

[6] See also Feidelson, *Symbolism in American Literature*, pp. 126–27.

or externized—it is no thought (*J*, IX, 175; *W*, XII, 41; *W*, IV, 264).
The desire for knowledge unaccompanied by the desire to use it, to
receive but not to give, he regards as base and potentially monstrous
(*W*, III, 269–70; *W*, II, 113). Health consists in the faithful application of influences from the universal to the particuar, in the successful
combination of the speculative and the practical (*W*, I, 208–9; *W*,
IV, 267–68). Therefore in action, in transition, is man's power; but
action is not to be confused with pointless activity. It is a twofold
process: the transition of a thought from the unconscious to the
conscious, and the implementation of the thought in a form. This is
an alternating process, one activity generating the other: forms
stimulate thought, and thought stimulates the creation of new forms
(*W*, II, 163; *W*, I, 94–95, 22–23).[7]

The transmission of influences from the vast to the particular requires concentration. This involves the danger of narrowness, to
be sure, but if the individual follows the polarity of the intellect—
uses his action as a means of stimulating new thought—such danger
is averted, for new thought is an expansion, a step to a generalization
ordering a larger class of facts (*W*, VI, 75; *W*, XII, 51, 58; *W*, V,
239). Expansion is necessary for growth, while concentration is necessary for the successful transformation of power into form; the greater the expansion, or insight, and the greater the concentration, the
completeness of the distillation, the more successful, enduring, and
useful will be the form (*W*, I, 88).

We have already discussed the creation of social forms, but another
mode of expressing the higher intellect is the intellectual form or
system, particularly in philosophy and theology. Each proceeds from
an insight, an intuition of the nature of reality, or man, or the relation of man to God, etc., and each is the outcome of a deliberate
ordering of the intuition into a comprehensible form, a verbaliza-
tion of an extrasensible fact. As such each is the expression of a perception, and since thought must be expressed to be a thought at all,
the intellectual form is necessary. It is also necessary, of course, as
a means of communicating the insight; otherwise, the insight could
have no social significance. But Emerson, while conceding the necessity for philosophy and theology, distrusts their effectiveness as
forms expressing the perceptions of the reason. Their formal basis

---

[7] Compare C. S. Peirce's conception that pragmatism "is correct doctrine only
in so far as it is recognized that material action is the mere husk of ideas. . . . But
the end of thought is action only in so far as the end of action is another
thought." Quoted by Carpenter, "William James and Emerson," p. 45. At the
base of this conception, of course, is the organic idea of the necessity for growth.

is consistency of a logical sort, and he does not feel that the human mind can construct a consistent system that is not a "vain attempt to introvert and analyze the Primal Thought" (*W*, XII, 12).

The main reasons for Emerson's distrust of logic are linguistic and epistemological. We need to recall his theory of the relation between language and reality: words signify natural facts; particular natural facts are symbols of particular spiritual facts; and nature as a whole is the symbol of spirit (*W*, I, 25). This means that to represent or express—indeed, even to be aware of[8]—our thoughts, emotions, or anything of an intangible nature, we have had to adapt words representing physical phenomena as symbols. Even when we think language is being used literally the terms are figurative, for language is a structure of images or tropes, which in their secondary use no longer remind us of their metaphoric origin (*W*, III, 22). Consequently there is a necessary imprecision in language: words "cannot cover the dimensions of what is in truth. They break, chop, and impoverish it" (*W*, I, 45). Words are finite organs that can get at truth from only one side. But truth is infinite, with innumerable sides (*W*, I, 44).

As a contemporary of Emerson's, Horace Bushnell, explains, the logician's fallacy stems from his infinite reliance on the finite organs; he must define, for example, with the greatest precision, yet definitions actually involve only changes of symbol, and if we take them to be literal truth, they infallibly lead us into error. The logician, accepting his definitions as literally true, makes a consistent deduction leading to a conclusion that renders the syllogism false—"false, because of its consistency";[9] false because, as Emerson puts it, "if a man fasten his attention on a single aspect of truth and apply himself to that alone for a long time, the truth becomes distorted and not itself but falsehood" (*W*, II, 339). For these reasons Emerson complains that metaphysics are somewhat "surgical" (*W*, XII, 14), and confesses "to a little distrust of that completeness of system that metaphysicians are apt to affect. 'T is the gnat grasping the world" (*W*, XII, 12). Such systems impose barriers on the unbounded, unboundable essence called truth (*W*, I, 108). "That essence refuses to be recorded in propositions" (*W*, I, 62).[10]

---

[8] See Chapter I, pp. 4–5.

[9] *God in Christ. Three Discourses, Delivered at New Haven, Cambridge, and Andover, with a Preliminary Dissertation on Language* (Hartford: Hartford, Brown and Parsons, 1849), pp. 72, 57.

[10] Jonathan Bishop indicates this drawback to intellectual forms quite aptly: "Classification has its negative side as well. A circle turned substantial and confining is a wall. This image...will also apply to all intellectual situations

As Emerson phrases it elsewhere, "when the Muse is wanting, the student is prone to supply its place with microscopic subtleties and logomachy," but when one ceases to report his intuition of truth and attempts to correct and contrive it, it is no longer truth (*W*, X, 306; *W*, II, 329). The truth suffers because the contrivance results in an excess of form; the dynamic, vital quality of life is transformed into a condition of stasis (*W*, IV, 133). A man simply trusts in his intuitions, finally—Emerson is under no illusion that they are always scientifically or philosophically verifiable—and faith cannot be proven by syllogisms (*W*, VIII, 346). The perceptions of the reason cannot be fully comprehended or taught by the understanding: to it, for example, the utterances of Christ in the Sermon on the Mount are nonsense (*W*, I, 129; *J*, III, 236–37). Yet philosophy and theology deliberately attempt to explain the reason's facts solely in terms of the understanding, and therein lies their basic weakness.

Another weakness stems from the tendency—among those whom the forms are designed to assist—to trust the system as an end, as the truth itself, rather than as a means of communicating or realizing the truth. This transference of reverence from the truth to the expression becomes, then, a limitation, and the form itself becomes an imposition, a barrier to growth (*W*, I, 88–89; *W*, II, 80):

> We have our theory of life, our religion, our philosophy; and the event of each moment, the shower, the steamboat disaster, the passing of a beautiful face, the apoplexy of our neighbor, are all tests to try our theory, the approximate result we call truth, and reveal its defects. If I have renounced the search of truth, if I have come into the port of some pretending dogmatism, some new church or old church, some Schelling or Cousin, I have died to all use of these new events that are born out of prolific time into multitude of life every hour. (*W*, X, 132–33)

Men have a choice between truth and repose—between growth and stagnation—and all too often they choose repose (*W*, II, 341–42). And philosophy and theology do not correct this basic tendency.

Men must consider the originators of intellectual systems not as original powers in themselves, but as effects and channels of universal power; and consider their creations not as truth, or as complete systemizations of truth, but as partial expressions of truth that can stimulate their own growth (*W*, IV, 34–35). Then they will realize that although the expressions are faulty, although the expressors are finite, the truth itself stands, flawless and infinite (*W*, X,

---

in which a single set of terms, a single classification, has begun to constrict the experience of a mind that originally expressed its native freedom by establishing it." *Emerson on the Soul*, p. 55.

195–96). But truth is not something appropriate merely for remote appreciation. It is, ultimately, God's order, and the perception of it should stimulate the desire to live and die for it. In a moral context, religion should thus be the desire not only to do all good, but for the sake of the good to suffer all evil. But Emerson is convinced that for this purpose—that of stimulating such desires—not only are the old creeds outgrown, but a technical intellectual system is unsuitable (*W*, V, 231; *W*, VIII, 329; *W*, XI, 478). The form should serve both as an expression of power and as a means to action, and the intellectual system proves unsatisfactory because it partially fulfills at best only the former.

Emerson considered science to be an intellectual form as well as a technique, the purpose of which was, through the search for resemblance and identity, to enlarge not only men's power over physical phenomena, but also their comprehension of the corresponding laws of matter and mind (*W*, VIII, 7–8; *W*, VI, 284; *W*, X, 130). But he did not feel that the science of his time was fulfilling its purpose: its metaphysical basis was narrowly materialistic, its concentration was exclusively on materialistic ends, and its discoveries were consequently of a superficial nature, insufficient to improve the quality of men's lives (*W*, VI, 284; *W*, III, 14). Its theories of truth were solely the result of inductive and deductive reasoning applied to data derived from analyses of isolated phenomena. By not being poetic, by discounting the valid use of intuition, this method could not produce the profound insights into nature and man that were the true end of science (*W*, V, 253–54, 239–40; *W*, VIII, 10). Emerson, it should be noted, was complaining that science, as commonly practiced, was incapable of producing general theories such as those of gravitation, evolution, relativity, and so forth. And it was such theories—those that would increase knowledge of the basic laws of nature and man, and of their relation to one another and to God—that he desired. He longed for and demanded a science of poetic and religious value (*W*, VIII, 211, 220–21; *W*, XII, 5).[11]

[11] Whitehead has the same misgivings for much the same reason, which he makes admirably clear: "In regard to the aesthetic needs of civilized society the reactions of science have so far been unfortunate. Its materialistic basis has directed attention to *things* as opposed to *values*. The antithesis is a false one, if taken in a concrete sense. But it is valid at the abstract level of ordinary thought. This misplaced emphasis coalesced with the abstractions of political economy, which are in fact the abstractions in terms of which commercial affairs are carried on. Thus all thought concerned with social organization expressed itself in terms of material things and of capital. Ultimate values were excluded. They were politely bowed to and then handed over to the clergy to be kept for Sundays. A creed of competitive business morality was evolved,

Emerson hopes in particular for a new affirmative statement of life and duty that will reconcile and transcend the previous basic beliefs of men (*W*, III, 75; *W*, VI, 240–42). But neither philosophy nor science, he suspects, can produce such a statement. Because of their exclusive reliance on the intellectual faculties, they create the disparity between subject and object that prevents the wholeness of experience necessary for the perception and communication of truth (*W*, IV, 76; *W*, XII, 14; *W*, VIII, 10). But he believes that such an approach exists in art, particularly in poetry. In Thoreau's words, "Poetry *implies* the whole truth. Philosophy *expresses* a particle of it."[12] Thought alone attempts to discover unity through unity—hence its partiality—whereas poetry attempts the same thing through the variety of material phenomena, thereby enabling itself to cope with the many-faceted unity of truth (*W*, IV, 56; *W*, II, 312–313).

In Emerson's view, the only difference between the philosopher (or the scientist) and the poet is that the former's immediate aim is truth, the latter's beauty. The philosopher seeks the unconditioned, absolute basis of conditional, phenomenal existence on the faith that such a basis exists in laws that are the absolute determinants of phenomena. According to Emerson's doctrine of correspondence, these laws, when in the mind, are ideas, and are infinitely beautiful. Beauty is the aesthetic face of truth, truth the cognitive face of beauty. Therefore, the true philosopher and the true poet should be one and the same, and their goal should be the perception and creation of a beauty that is truth and a truth that is beauty (*W*, I, 55).[13]

The poet's task is central to human life because the world is wholly beautiful and is the creation of beauty (*W*, III, 7). Because they are part of the system of nature, all men are stimulated by their perceptions of beauty to reproduce in their own right new forms expressing those perceptions. But not many have the constructive ability to create, and the poet fulfills this need for them. The poet provides them with a vicarious experience of creation that is essential for their health (*W*, XII, 218–19; *W*, III, 5–6; *W*, VIII, 247–48).

Emerson never attempts to define beauty, but he lists a few of its

---

in some respects curiously high; but entirely devoid of consideration for the value of human life. The workmen were conceived as mere hands, drawn from the pool of labour." *Science and the Modern World*, pp. 291–92.

[12] Quoted by Matthiessen, *American Renaissance*, p. 85.

[13] The following analysis is generally indebted to Norman Foerster's presentation of Emerson's aesthetic theory in *American Criticism: A Study in Literary Theory from Poe to the Present* (Boston: Houghton Mifflin, 1928), especially p. 59.

qualities: "We ascribe beauty to that which is simple; which has no superfluous parts; which exactly answers its end; which stands related to all things; which is the mean of many extremes." Its qualities are the most enduring and most ascending (*W*, VI, 289). These are also qualities of nature, so that forms of beauty, by virtue of their subordination to ideal nature, are continuations, and never contradictions, of the laws of nature; like natural phenomena, they are products of the universal mind (*W*, VII, 48). Emerson approves of Goethe's definition of beauty—"The beautiful is a manifestation of secret laws of nature, which, but for this appearance, had been forever concealed from us"—and in his own words describes it as "the instant dependence of form upon soul" (*W*, VI, 288; *W*, III, 3).

Beauty is the expression through form of power, of the deepest and simplest attributes of human nature, and it is intelligible only to those men who are aware of these attributes. Forms as such are not beautiful, nor is beauty as such in the forms themselves. It is a synthesis of cosmically related qualities expressed by the form and perceived by the mind, which itself shares those qualities (*W*, II, 351, 359; *W*, VI, 303). Beauty properly rests in power—the power of the universal mind, the corresponding power in men's minds, the ideal order of nature—but the form is necessary to express and apprehend it. "We do not enclose watches in wooden, but in crystal cases," Emerson says, "and rhyme is the transparent frame that allows almost the pure architecture of thought to become visible to the mental eye. Substance is much, but so are mode and form much" (*W*, VIII, 52–53).

Poetry is fundamental, healthy, and wise, because it stems from and embodies the perception that the origin of phenomena is spiritual power. It expresses the real informing the apparent, and thus reveals their proper relationship. "As a power it is the perception of the symbolic character of things, and the treating them as representative: as a talent it is a magnetic tenaciousness of an image, and by the treatment demonstrating that this pigment [*sic*] of thought is as palpable and objective to the poet as is the ground on which he stands, or the walls of houses about him" (*W*, VIII, 27). In terms of the artistic process itself, creation springs from a balance of inspiration and discipline, of involuntary and voluntary activities.[14]

The success or completeness of poetic expression, its conformity with nature, depends upon the depth of the poet's insight into the objects depicted (*W*, II, 355). Insight, a function of the imagination,

[14] Foerster recognizes this same point. See "Emerson on the Organic Principle in Art," *PMLA* 41 (1926): 203.

pierces below the surface of phenomena to perceive the true relation between material fact and idea, to see the organic relation of natural phenomena to one another, to man, and to God (*W*, VIII, 28–29). This perception is not an invention, but a discovery—creation is properly discovery—and accordingly Emerson believes that the best aspects of a work of art, the universal qualities, are the product more of nature than of the individual artist (*W*, VII, 47–48).

The artist, as the creator in the finite, gets his power from the universal mind, which is *the* creator, by ridding himself of his egotism and willfulness, by submitting the energy of his own intellect, the understanding, to the nature of things, the reason (*W*, VII, 48–49, 50–51; *W*, III, 26–27).[15] Such a perception or thought exerts a great pressure to be expressed. In Martin Buber's terms, there exists a necessity to render an I-Thou into an I-It relation. By expressing it the artist actually expresses himself, that is "his proper character" or higher self; submission to the reason is synonymous with genuine self-expression (*W*, VII, 56; *W*, II, 360). In the creative process, ideally all the temporal aspects connected both with the fact perceived and the perceiver are shed; the perception stimulates the creation of a form new and universal (*W*, IV, 215; *W*, III, 24). Art, however, is not an involuntary process. It is the creation of forms by means of the power of the universal mind, to be sure, and relative to that mind all creation, even that of animals, we can call art. But relative to themselves the animals' activity is instinctive, whereas men's activity is the spirit's voluntary creation of forms (*W*, VII, 39).

The artist must attempt to make his perceptions meaningful to the whole man, emotion and thought, the understanding as well as the reason, lest they be too vague and indefinite for application to men's lives (*W*, I, 182). He must be a man immersed in his own age, for he must employ contemporary symbols in order to convey his perception to others; and he must be immersed in the literature of the past, for tradition provides him with materials and conventions necessary for successful communication. Art is not a creation of some-

---

[15] Emerson bases this principle—call it the muse—on experience, an experience common to creative people. Compare, for instance, Paul Klee's statement in a lecture, "On Modern Art," delivered at Jena in 1924: "chosen are those artists who penetrate to the region of that secret place where primeval power nurtures all evolution. . . . There, where the powerhouse of all time and space—call it brain or heart of creation—activates every function; who is the artist who would not dwell there? In the womb of nature, at the source of creation, where the secret key to all lies guarded." Quoted by T. M. Brown, "Greenough, Paine, Emerson and the Organic Aesthetic," *Journal of Aesthetics and Art Criticism* 14 (1956): 313.

thing entirely new *ex nihilo*; it is the transformation of temporal common facts into a new combination or form within conventions, a form rendering facts into images or metaphors universally expressive of a truth, the poet's original perception (*W*, II, 352; *W*, IV, 189, 194). The artist, moreover, without mistaking his images as ends, can never ignore or slight them for their meaning (*W*, V, 234): "The poet, like the electric rod, must reach from a point nearer the sky than all surrounding objects, down to the earth, and into the dark wet soil, or neither is of use. The poet must not only converse with pure thought, but he must demonstrate it almost to the senses. His words must be pictures, his verses must be spheres and cubes, to be seen and smelled and handled. His fable must be a good story, and its meaning must hold as pure truth" (*W*, XII, 366). Fulfilling the functions of art, Emerson indicates, requires an exacting discipline of the physical, intellectual, and moral faculties (*W*, XII, 243).

The power in art comes from the intuitive principle of the reason, from the universal mind, which the artist allows to work through him. But submitting to the reason and expressing its perceptions are voluntary acts of the will. This process is the artistic equivalent of losing oneself to find oneself, and requires great discipline and hard work. To be sure, Emerson sometimes (too often) overstates his conception of art as a spontaneous product of the universal mind: "No, what has been best done in the world,—the works of genius,— cost nothing. There is no painful effort, but it is the spontaneous flowing of the thought. Shakespeare made his Hamlet as a bird weaves its nest. Poems have been written between sleeping and waking, irresponsibly" (*W*, VII, 181–82).[16] On the other hand he indicates (in regrettable prose) that the achievement of spontaneity can be difficult and arduous: "Doubt not, O poet, but persist. Say, It is in me, and shall out. Stand there, balked and dumb, stuttering and stammering, hissed and hooted, stand and strive, until at last rage draw out of thee that *dream*-power which every night shows thee is thine own" (*W*, III, 40). He can also say, on occasion, that the act of expression itself requires concentration, effort, and the practical mastery of tools acquired through drill and discipline (*W*, II, 336; *W*, X, 144, 147); and his sharp complaints to and with Ellery Channing for his

[16] This type of statement led to Vivian Hopkins's observation that the principal lack in Emerson's aesthetic theory is an explanation of the transference of an intuition into objective form. *Spires of Form: A Study of Emerson's Aesthetic Theory* (Cambridge, Mass.: Harvard University Press, 1951), p. 137. It is a lack, no doubt, but on the other hand no one has explained how this is done, no more than how an intuition occurs. The act of creation remains a mystery, otherwise the creation of art would be much easier and more predictable.

disdain of craft (not to speak of his own method of writing) indicate that in private Emerson insists on utterly deliberate composition (*J*, VI, 46, 357–59; *J*, IX, 54).[17] In the midst of such conflicting statements, it is apparent to me that while Emerson is aware of the necessity for careful deliberation, he wishes to stress that the insights and ideas for art, as for any other activity, come and must come spontaneously: "We do not determine what we will think. We only open our senses, clear away as we can all obstruction from the fact, and suffer the intellect to see" (*W*, II, 328). Quite simply, good ideas cannot be contrived.

The poet uses images as figures or illustrations of his thought or insight, and thereby he creates symbols, which all men must have (*W*, VIII, 11; *W*, VII, 212). An insight, in fact, always realizes itself in an image, for it is a law of nature that spirit incarnates itself; and the better the mastery of the insight—the better the understanding of the principle, its implications, its relation to material phenomena—the more appropriate and meaningful the symbol will be. Therefore a good symbol is evidence of the keenness of one's thought; in itself it indicates the truth of the thought, its basic accord with nature. For that reason, symbols are the most effective means of communication and persuasion (*W*, VIII, 17–18, 13).

The symbol is possible—and powerful—because phenomena are symbols and nature itself is a symbol, a realization of universal power (*W*, VIII, 15, 20; *W*, III, 13). The facts in nature are nouns of the intellect—they correspond to thoughts of the mind—and have manifold uses and meanings, because every natural phenomenon corresponds to a fact in man's mental experience, and the fact in his experience corresponds to many natural phenomena. His perception of the phenomenon is itself a fact. If his mental experience is profound and if he treats it honestly, he transforms the natural fact into a symbol of universal significance and meaning, for his thought is true both to nature and to other men (*W*, VI, 304; *W*, VIII, 271; *W*, II, 65; *W*, VIII, 29–30, 34–35). Thus he uses language properly, deliberately creating symbols with symbols.

In order to be organic and universal, the symbol must not be static, must not be rigidly expressive of a particular idea (which is a basic flaw of philosophic and theological expression). "In nature, each individual symbol plays innumerable parts, as each particle of matter circulates in turn through every system" (*W*, IV, 120–21; *W*, III, 34–35). The poet attempts to express the perception that the object is always "flowing" in an ascending metamorphosis and simultaneously that the origin of the form, spiritual power, is permanent,

17 *Letters*, 2: 252–53; 3: 102–3.

yet acts as the force impelling the form's flow—in short, its becoming and being, respectively.[18] And he accomplishes this by using "forms according to the life, and not according to the form" (*W*, VIII, 15, 17; *W*, III, 21). With such an organic conception Emerson is trying to discourage allegory—a particular meaning attached to a particular image—and encourage the use of symbols that are dynamic, capable of multiple meaning, of paradox, of manifold suggestion and implication, like Melville's whale, Keats's nightingale, and Stevens's pineapple.

Similarly, artistic structure should also be organic—not bounded or rigid—but dynamically expressing its own informing life, and exhibiting that life by suggesting transition, as if it were ready to flow into other forms. "The interruption of equilibrium stimulates the eye to desire the restoration of symmetry, and to watch the steps through which it is attained" (*W*, VI, 292). In accordance with Emerson's list of the qualities of beauty, the form must be without extraneous embellishment, without any suggestion of caprice, and should be perfectly expressive of the thought or intuition, that is, of the particular manifestation of the universal mind, just as the plant is expressive of the seed (*W*, VII, 50, 53; *W*, XII, 303–4): "For it is not metres, but a metre-making argument that makes a poem,—a thought so passionate and alive that like the spirit of a plant or an animal it has an architecture of its own, and adorns nature with a new thing" (*W*, III, 9–10). From this statement we see the dual sense of the word *organic* that Emerson uses: the relative depth of the poet's intuition, and the degree of success with which he concretely expresses the intuition.[19] But the organic conception is an ideal as well, for in Emerson's view no insight has been as deep as it might have been, and no expression has attained the perfection seen in nature. Elements of the local and ephemeral are always present; man *is* a creator in the finite (*W*, II, 362–63; *W*, VII, 37).

Finally, we should consider one further implication of Emerson's

[18] As Vivian Hopkins states: "Emerson thinks of the symbol as having effect not so much through perfect fusion of idea with image, as through the expression given to the object by the idea, in the moment of flowing through it. The idea may remain in the reader's mind, or the object may be put to fresh uses by the poet; but idea and image are not considered as inseparably fused in a new unity. The material object has only temporary value, in objectifying spiritual intuition. As the spirit flows on, it leaves the object behind." *Spires of Form*, pp. 130–31. But this does not mean that the form is unimportant or unnecessary, as Gene Bluestein has pointed out: "Emerson's Epiphanies," *New England Quarterly* 39 (1966): 452–56.

[19] As pointed out by Foerster, *American Criticism*, p. 64, and Matthiessen, *American Renaissance*, p. 135.

organicism that he clearly sees and affirms: art "differs from the works of Nature in this, that they are organically reproductive. This [i.e., art] is not, but spiritually it is prolific by its powerful action on the intellects of men" (*W*, VII, 51). Art should be another aspect of nature; those forms of art that are not organic, that are distinct from and contrary to nature, he characterizes as forms of death, for they are not alive, moving, and reproductive (*W*, II, 365, 367–68).[20] But so to conceive of art frankly makes it, not immaculately self-contained in form, but initial, a favorite Emersonian word (*W*, II, 362). It must be judged by its effect, for its organic purpose is to have an effect. And it is in part by its effect that it demonstrates its superiority to other intellectual forms.

Poetry is the consolation of mortal men, but not an asylum from the evils of their life. Men are imprisoned by their old modes of thought and employment; they live in the midst of and are dominated by powers that they call fate. The poet loosens their chains, frees and consoles them by transporting them to a higher point of vantage and showing a larger generalization by which they can understand these limiting facts. Thereby are they reconciled, lifted above fate to power, to voluntary obedience to necessity (*W*, II, 366; *W*, VIII, 37–38; *W*, III, 12, 18, 33).

Emerson considers the greatest contribution of Swedenborg and Wordsworth to be the reunion of nature and mind, the divorce of which made nature suspect and poetry superficial (*W*, VIII, 66). Organic poetry leads us to phenomenal and metaphysical nature, physical facts and moral facts, and reveals their relationship, the applicability of the ideal and moral to the affairs of the moment. Thinking of Plato as a poet, Emerson says that he built a bridge from the streets of cities to Atlantis (*W*, XII, 315; *W*, VIII, 31–32; *W*, IV, 61).

Since the finest poetry is the product of the universal mind, it is universal and ultimately religious in meaning (*W*, II, 358). Its supreme value, therefore, is to educate men to a height beyond itself, to stimulate men to order and virtue (*W*, VIII, 65–66). Emerson wants to reunite art and religion (*W*, X, 249), to make art a form of religious experience, and he wants religion to inform the conduct of life. Hence he conceives of art as initial, not as an end in itself (*W*, IV, 211; *J*, V, 398–99).[21] Still, he regards art as necessary, and as the

[20] Hence Richard Poirer's acute statement that for Emerson "Art is an action, not a product of action." *A World Elsewhere: The Place of Style in American Literature* (New York: Oxford University Press, 1966), p. 21.

[21] On this point, see Lawrence I. Buell, "Unitarian Poetics and Emerson's Poet-priest," *American Quarterly* 20 (1968): 20; and Wendell Glick, "The Moral and Ethical Dimensions of Emerson's Aesthetic," *ESQ*, No. 55 (1969): 13–14.

best—because the most inclusive and justly proportioned—available intellectual form, a form demonstrating the proper relationship of power and form in theme and structure, stimulating an essential attitude toward life .

> Subtle rhymes, with ruin rife,
> Murmur in the house of life,
> Sung by the Sisters as they spin;
> In perfect time and measure they
> Build and unbuild our echoing clay
> As the two twilights of the day
> Fold us music-drunken in.
> (*W*, IX, 124)

He wishes not to belittle the importance of art, but rather to define its importance within a cosmic scale of values. As Emerson is primarily a religious writer, one can hardly expect him to place art in any other perspective.

All forms created by men are initial. In order to grow, all men must learn everything for themselves, and because we must experience a fact to know it, we cannot blandly accept as valid the codified forms and rules of the past (*W*, I, 127; *J*, IV, 306). However, rather than ignore them we must study and test them (*W*, IV, 172). We need the forms of the past, our cultural heritage—of which we are inescapably products—because it is only by virtue of this inheritance that we can fully realize our own latent powers of mind and soul (*W*, VIII, 200, 217). "The Past is for us; but the sole terms on which it can become ours are its subordination to the Present. . . . We must not tamper with the organic motion of the Soul. . . . This vast memory is only raw material. The divine gift is ever the instant life, which receives and uses and creates, and can well bury the old in the omnipotency with which Nature decomposes all her harvest for recomposition" (*W*, VIII, 204). Our power comes from transition, from movement from the old to the new by means of facts, and it is power derived from past intellectual forms that Emerson—like Thoreau, Whitman, Louis Sullivan, Paul Goodman—wants, the inspiration or stimulation as well as the discipline to attain and use our own power (*W*, XII, 59, 13; *W*, I, 89). He desires originality, which he defines as "being, being one's self, and reporting accurately what we see and are" (*W*, VIII, 201). We must first of all be; the reporting can take various forms, the most important of which is our mode of living. This mode, an inseparable union of being and doing, he calls character.

The most significant problem we face is essence—the questions of whence, what, and whither. Books provide approximate and oblique solutions, of necessity, but living offers a direct solution (*W*, IV, 94). To live is a man's basic resource, a total act; thinking is a function of living, and is a partial act. Character, therefore, is superior to intellect (*W*, I, 99). Since character is the source of all our activity and works, we should center our interest in it, as cause, rather than in effects (*W*, VII, 185). Therefore the proper object of our existence is the education of the will (*W*, VII, 275).

The educated will is aligned with the reason of things, is one with nature, is the domestication of the moral order in the individual. It denotes a habitual self-possession that is the outcome of a constant regard for interior and constitutional motives, and which cannot be distracted by outward events because with it one acts not from mixed motives but always from one constant motive (*W*, III, 95–96; *W*, X, 102). That motive, which is the highest form of beauty, is a voluntary obedience to God's law on the moral level, a necessitated freedom. When a man's "mind is illuminated, when his heart is kind, he throws himself joyfully into the sublime order, and does, with knowledge, what the stones do by structure" (*W*, X, 55; *W*, VI, 240). Moral action—to mend oneself—is the essence of our freedom and power because that is the one thing, Emerson always insists, we really can do (*W*, X, 208; *J*, III, 423; *W*, I, 41, 64, 73; *W*, VI, 240; further, this notion of freedom informs all of the "Divinity School Address"). The motive that properly makes an action moral, in a nonreligious context, is the direction of the will toward universal rather than private ends. Emerson subscribes to Kant's axiom, "Act always so that the immediate motive of thy will may become a universal rule for all intelligent beings," because it also defines how to apply the absolute law of the moral sentiment to a relative world (*W*, X, 92; *W*, VII, 27).

It is significant that Emerson stresses the motivation of action. He takes great care in his ethics to keep the distinction between good and evil as clear and firm as possible. Within the framework of his conception of nature, in which all evil necessarily becomes productive of good, there is the danger of losing the need to distinguish, from a utilitarian position, between a good and an evil act. Emerson is aware of the danger, and thus he rejects a utilitarian ethic—according to which one judges an act by its intended result—for an intuitionist ethic, whereby one judges an act by its motivation. In the words of Eliot, "The last temptation is the greatest treason:/To do the right deed for the wrong reason."[22] Emerson, consequently, insists that

---

[22] *Murder in the Cathedral* (London: Faber, 1935), p. 44.

self-interest can never prompt a sincere service of others (yet one can intend a good result for reasons of self-interest): a pure act, a truly virtuous act, requires a pure source.[23] One should aim not to be virtuous, but to be virtue (*W*, I, 121). Only in this way, within his cosmos, can Emerson keep a sharp distinction.

But a problem arises here concerning the proper form of the virtuous life. Emerson shares in large part the belief in a dualistic God characteristic of the western tradition of Platonism, a God Who, on the one hand, is perfect, self-contained, self-sufficient, out of time and space, and Who, on the other, is the creator, involved in the diversity of finite life in the limited temporal and spatial order. This dualism also extends to his conception of nature, which he characterizes as having self-equality, and yet as being in the process of evolution (*J*, VIII, 86). A. O. Lovejoy has defined the ethical implications of this conception of God.

With this theological dualism—since the idea of God was taken to be also the definition of the highest good—there ran...a dualism of values, the one other-worldly (though often in a half-hearted way), the other this-worldly. If the good for man was the contemplation or the imitation of God, this required, on the one hand, a transcendence and suppression of the merely "natural" interests and desires, a withdrawal of the soul from "the world" the better to prepare it for the beatific vision of the divine perfection; and it required, on the other hand, a piety towards the God of things as they are, an adoring delight in the sensible universe in all its variety, an endeavor on man's part to know and understand it ever more fully, and a conscious participation in the divine activity of creation.[24]

To the degree Emerson accepts the theological dualism, he is confronted with the ethical dualism. His ethical doctrine offers, however, not a choice between the ethical values, but, characteristically, a resolution. He renders the duality polar.

He says that the highest achievement of man is self-existence, for Deity is self-existent (*W*, I, 334-35), and elsewhere he remarks—in what could be called a definition of self-existence—that "that which the soul seeks is resolution into being above form, out of Tartarus, and out of heaven,—liberation from nature" (*W*, IV, 51). Such a resolution, like Nicholas of Cusa's description of God as a circle

---

[23] *Young Emerson Speaks*, p. 128. In *The Nature of True Virtue*, Jonathan Edwards uses the same ethic to prove man's innate depravity. Interestingly both insist that a truly virtuous act indicates the presence of God in the soul. It is in their definition of God's mode of action, of His relation to man, that they essentially differ.

[24] *The Great Chain of Being*, p. 316.

whose circumference is nowhere and whose center is everywhere, can be called a definition either of formlessness or of absolute form.

> Higher far into the pure realm,
> Over sun and star,
> Over the flickering Daemon film,
> Thou must mount for love;
> Into vision where all form
> In the only form dissolves.
>   (*W*, IX, 115)

Emerson exhibits, at times, a clear sympathy for the otherworldly ideal: "Mankind have such a deep stake in inward illumination, that there is much to be said by the hermit or monk in defence of his life of thought and prayer. A certain partiality, a headiness and loss of balance, is the tax which all action must pay. Act, if you like,—but you do it at your peril. Men's actions are too strong for them. Show me a man who has acted and who has not been the victim and slave of his action. What they have done commits and enforces them to do the same again. The first act, which was to be an experiment, becomes a sacrament" (*W*, IV, 266–67). And therefore Emerson constantly distinguishes between a man and his actions, and values the man more as spirit, the source of power, than as actor, the agent of power, because actions tend to commit the agent and thereafter limit his power.

But Emerson also stresses the relative superiority of integrity to action, of being to doing, because with integrity one will not be mastered by one's means. One can still act, but in a different way and for different reasons. "Every man takes care that his neighbor shall not cheat him. But a day comes when he begins to care that he do not cheat his neighbor" (*W*, VI, 277–78, 215–16). Emerson's emphasis on being is not intended as an other-worldly ideal, but as exhortation to realign action with moral nature, to encourage acting according to one self-sufficient motive rather than many motives imposed by external events; in short, one should act from within instead of without (*W*, X, 224–25). Opposed to other-direction, to use David Reisman's terms, Emerson encourages inner-direction, and he attempts to define how, in the dissolution of common beliefs and values, it can be attained.

In mundane terms action is necessary for survival, but in moral terms it is a duty. The great vice of men who find themselves participating in faulty, sinful institutions, even if they favor reform, is that they nevertheless do not feel personally accountable for the condition of the institutions: "no one feels himself called to act for man, but only as a fraction of man" (*W*, III, 58; *W*, X, 198–99; *W*, I, 233). The middle measure of our being is best; between the extremes of pure intellect and pure sensation is the equator of human activity, where mind and matter are united in action (*W*, III, 62).

In his definition of religion and ethics Emerson emphasizes the need for action: the former he conceives of as the system of human duties commencing from God, the latter, duties from man; both essentially consist in the practice of ideas, or the introduction of ideas into life (*W*, I, 58). Truth is the summit of man's being, and justice is the application of it to his affairs (*W*, III, 95; *W*, IV, 290). The aim is not to be virtuous, but to be virtue; yet virtue is adherence in action to the nature of things, the implementation of the dictates of the universal mind by the individual will; and the habit of this adherence is character. In Emerson's view, to act in this way is to be: "In a virtuous action I properly *am*" (W, II, 122). In that action that is not only virtuous, in the common sense, but is also an expression of virtue—motivated strictly by a concern for universal ends—being and doing are no longer distinguishable. Each informs the other and, in effect, becomes the other (*W*, X, 197–98; *W*, II, 160).[25] As Emerson says in the "Divinity School Address," "the intuition of the moral sentiment is an insight of the perfection of the laws of the soul. These laws execute themselves. . . . He who does a good deed is instantly ennobled. He who does a mean deed is by the action itself contracted" (*W*, I, 122). Hence Emerson's imperative to "do right now"; the individual, being responsible for his own condition, cannot escape his own past. The force of character is cumulative, so that the habit of badness makes goodness increasingly difficult, whereas the habit of goodness makes it increasingly easy (*W*, II, 59; *W*, VI, 13).

To act from the intuition of the moral sentiment is to act in accordance with moral nature and with infinite power, for the will then cannot be diverted by any external pressure (*W*, VI, 28–29). The success of the action, in common terms, is irrelevant; the act can still be the expression of virtue, and to Emerson virtue is enough.

[25] Sherman Paul makes much the same point in a slightly different context: "Experience, transformed into ideas by the symbolization of the mind, had to be enacted by informing the conduct of life. For Emerson the aim of life was to extend the inner order one achieved by his angle of vision to the outward, active order of character: on the level of the actual, the quest of reality became the quest of character; and inversely, the quest of character through action became the quest of reality. If expression was most naturally realized by unfolding ideas after the pattern of the chain of being, similarly man best developed character by living that unfolding, by rising through the chain, from sensually to spiritually directed behavior." *Emerson's Angle of Vision*, p. 133.

It is its own reward, and therefore the man of virtue can abide any loss (*W*, II, 255). "We perish, and perish gladly, if the law remains" (*W*, X, 195). It is in this sense—that virtue is enough—that the aim of life should be self-sufficiency or self-existence. "To a well-principled man existence is victory" (*W*, X, 121). And it is in this sense that Emerson advocates acquiescence and optimism.[26]

The individual, through the perpetual conflict between his personal interests and wishes, passions, and appetites, and the dictates of the universal mind, develops moral discipline by renouncing the private benefit and choosing to act toward universal ends (*W*, X, 94). In a very real sense, these lower impulses have a vital function in the moral life: "In general, every evil to which we do not succumb is a benefactor. As the Sandwich-Islander believes that the strength and valor of the enemy he kills passes into himself, so we gain the strength of the temptation we resist" (*W*, II, 118). Or, in Thoreau's words, "We cannot well do without our sins; they are the highway of our virtue."[27] As Josiah Royce develops the same idea, the virtuous act is a unit of experience consisting of two inseparable parts, the temptation to sin and the conquest of it.[28] But it must be understood that, as Emerson conceives it, this struggle is not between Manichean absolutes. Emerson agrees with Augustine that the personal drives that compose the temptation and create the struggle are necessary for survival as well as for stimulation of moral discipline; the purpose of the discipline is to transform their energy into morally useful courses. Divided from the discipline they are immoral; united with it they compose an integral part of moral action (*W*, VI, 254–55; *W*, XI, 155). Once again, the need is for self-knowledge, self-unification, and self-existence.[29]

The idea of disciplining drives into virtues accords with Emerson's "gradational" ethics. The virtue of self-subsistence, for example, can

[26] *The Correspondence of Thomas Carlyle and Ralph Waldo Emerson, 1834–1872*, ed. Charles E. Norton, rev., 1 (Boston, 1892): 367–68.

[27] Quoted by Foerster, *Nature in American Literature: Studies in the Modern View of Nature* (Boston: Russell & Russell, 1923), p. 133.

[28] *The Religious Aspect of Philosophy*, p. 454.

[29] Martin Buber postulates the same concept: The "evil urge" is necessary for survival, but it is evil only in so far as man has made it so by separating it from the moral urge. Man's duty is to reunite the two by subordinating the "evil" to the moral. Good and evil, therefore, are not diametrically opposed forces; evil is simply a lack of direction. *Good and Evil: Two Interpretations*, trans. Ronald Gregor Smith and Michael Bullock (New York: Scribner's, 1953), pp. 94–95, 97, 130–31.

be expressed in warfare, but at a higher level self-subsistence is enacted differently:

At a certain stage of his progress, the man fights, if he be of a sound body and mind. At a certain higher stage, he makes no offensive demonstration, but is alert to repel injury, and of an unconquerable heart. At a still higher stage, he comes into the region of holiness; passion has passed away from him; his warlike nature is all converted into an active medicinal principle; he sacrifices himself, and accepts with alacrity wearisome tasks of denial and charity; but, being attacked, he bears it and turns the other cheek, as one engaged, throughout his being, no longer to the service of an individual but to the common soul of all men. (*W*, XI, 166–67)

Each virtue can be transformed into a higher virtue—or, more precisely, the same virtue can be transformed into higher and higher modes of expression, according to an increasing understanding of the principle involved. That active transformation, of course, is organic growth (*W*, II, 314).[30]

Furthermore, at the lower levels the virtues, particularly self-subsistence, are inevitably competitive, but as they ascend they are less and less so, until finally, in "the region of holiness," there is, with no competition whatsoever, room for all (*W*, IV, 22; *W*, VIII, 301). At that level, life is a search for wisdom and virtue to the end of increasing wisdom and virtue, which all may share (*W*, II, 188).

The comcomitant of self-subsistence is self-responsibility. "When Duty whispers low, *Thou must,*/The youth replies, *I can*" (*W*, IX, 207). Because he can, he must; he has the power to obey, and so he has the responsibility.[31] Emerson does not dismiss the doctrine of total depravity in order to exculpate sinners; not to believe in it, the young minister stressed to his congregation, gives no one the excuse to "indulge in any practice that a stricter brother would condemn."[32] On the contrary, this dismissal has the effect of placing greater moral responsibility on the individual. Emerson's position is quite similar to that of Pelagius as Radoslav Tsanoff has defined it:

Too great emphasis on the inherent evil of our material nature involved certain moral hazards. "Human frailty" was apt to be used as an excuse for dissipation. The doughty virtue of the British monk Pelagius was outraged by the cowardly surrender which he found all too common. He

---

[30] Gray also indicated that Emerson's ethical theory is hierarchical. See *Emerson*, p. 73.

[31] See Whicher, *Freedom and Fate*, pp. 41–42, for a good analysis of this aspect of Emerson's ethics.

[32] *Young Emerson Speaks*, p. 232.

refused to admit that man's will lacked the power to fulfill what man's duty required. "If I ought, I can." In the name of liberty he denounced libertinism. God is just and will punish us for our evil deeds; our wills could have refrained from the evil, and we are thus responsible and blameworthy: so much for the sterner side of the Pelagian doctrine.[33]

Emerson, too, has a sterner side.

If a man has the power and therefore the responsibility to obey, then his enemies—the true forces of evil with which he must contend—are never external, but always within himself (*W*, X, 120). Accordingly, Emerson praises Goethe for stripping the Devil of his mythological gear and placing him where he belongs, in the mind of men (*W*, IV, 276–77). When a man fails to obey, when he breaks the laws of moral nature, like Dimmesdale and Ahab he loses his hold on the central reality, defeats the very end of his existence, deprives himself of his own true being or identity, and thereby renders his life a nothingness (*W*, VI, 322; *W*, XI, 237).

When he obeys, on the other hand, he acquires a living property that cannot be taken away (*W*, II, 88). Wisdom and virtue are proper additions of being; with them he rises at last into a region above sorrow, above tragedy, above any penalty (*W*, II, 122; *W*, XII, 417).[34] In the state of virtue, moreover, comes the perception and the reverence of the splendor of God bursting through every chink and cranny, the perception that the individual is dear to the heart of a God Who is beauty and goodness (*W*, II, 223; *W*, VII, 132–33, 306–7).

Martin Buber's conception of "reward and punishment" is strikingly similar to Emerson's. The wicked are punished here in that they have a revelation of their nothingness: "their nothingness has become their reality, the only being they have is their nothingness." Nothingness because they have, as Emerson expresses it, gone "out of acquaintance" with their own being (*W*, I, 122). The impure in heart lives, not in the truth, but "in the semblance of truth, where the fact that it 'goes ill' with him is confused with the illusion that God is not good to him." The pure in heart, on the other hand, has "in the end a direct experience of the Being of God," and perceives that God is good to him. "But this does not mean that God rewards

---

[33] *The Nature of Evil*, p. 40.

[34] As Jonathan Bishop puts it: "A truly good person is not miserable at all, but joyful; misery is by itself evidence that something is wrong inside, not merely outside. The self-righteous are unable to feel the reality of virtue. They see it as a rule exterior to themselves to which they must conform." Another indication, Emerson would say, that justice is done in this world, here and now. *Emerson on the Soul*, p. 73.

him with his goodness. It means, rather, that God's goodness is revealed to him who is pure in heart."[35] We attain our own being, ultimately, in the experience of God's being: "Blessed are the pure in heart: for they shall see God" (Matt., 5:8).

One experiences God's being as the outcome of attaining the state of virtue, which Emerson depicts as the acquisition of moral discipline through struggle. But he also depicts virtue as spontaneous (*W*, II, 133). In the same paragraph, however, he offers a key to the resolution of this possible contradiction by saying that a man's moral nature is vitiated by the interference of his will.[36] For in acquiring moral discipline, he acts for universal rather than private ends: he renounces his will for the universal will, but in renouncing he truly exercises his will, because this is a choice of the whole man: "I say, *do not choose*; but that is a figure of speech by which I would distinguish what is commonly called *choice* among men, and which is a partial act, the choice of the hands, of the eyes, of the appetites, and not a whole act of the man. But that which I call right or goodness, is the choice of my constitution" (*W*, II, 140). Such a choice Emerson calls spontaneous, in order to distinguish it from the common conception, which we might call impulsive. It means the attainment of a state of virtue, or character, in which, in a manner of speaking, the individual does not choose because his will is one with God's. It is comparable to the disciplined spontaneity of Thoreau and Zen Buddhism.

It is at this point that the man of religion resorts to paradox. For, as Tsanoff has written, it is here that the issue between self-fulfillment and self-denial loses any meaning, for utter self-denial is one with complete self-fulfillment.[37] Christ, of course, is the archetypal advocate in western tradition of this mode of fulfillment. "For whosoever exalteth himself shall be abased; and he that humbleth himself shall be exalted" (Luke, 14:11). Emerson too, throughout his career speaks of the height of lowliness (*W*, X, 194) and urges the value and practice of humility: "A man in the view of absolute goodness [the experience of God's Being], adores, with total humility. Every step so downward, is a step upward. The man who renounces himself, comes to himself" (*W*, I, 122). Christ says that "I can of mine own

---

[35] *Good and Evil*, pp. 12, 44, 34.

[36] See Gray, *Emerson*, pp. 74–75, and Bishop, *Emerson on the Soul*, pp. 66–72, for fine analyses of this ethical problem in Emerson's thought.

[37] See *The Nature of Evil*, pp. 383–87. Harold Fromm also affirms that for Emerson, self and impersonal spirit are not mutually exclusive but mutually necessary: "Emerson and Kierkegaard: The Problem of Historical Christianity," pp. 742–43.

self do nothing: as I hear, I judge: and my judgment is just; because I seek not mine own will, but the will of the Father which hath sent me" (John, 5:30). "Blessed be ye poor: for yours is the kingdom of God," He proclaims (Luke, 6:20), and later, "Whosoever shall seek to save his life shall lose it; and whosoever shall lose his life shall preserve it" (Luke, 17:33). Or, "Except a man be born again, he cannot see the kingdom of God" (John, 3:3). And in a parallel rush of paradoxes Emerson asserts that "by humility we rise, by obedience we command, by poverty we are rich, by dying we live" (*W*, X, 208). These statements of Emerson's should not suggest that he is somehow orthodox, theologically "sound," safe, but that he attempts to renew radical ideas as old as thought itself. They represent the fulfillment of self-reliance, which is comparable to the modern doctrines of Tillich's courage to be and Buber's one direction.

Tillich explains that the courage to be requires the surrender of our personal center to the logos of being, whereby there results an "identification of actual essence, power of being, and self-affirmation. ... The power of being is identified with virtue, and virtue consequently, with essential nature. Virtue is the power of acting exclusively according to one's true nature. And the degree of virtue is the degree to which somebody is striving for and able to affirm his own being."[38] And Buber explains that for the unified soul there is only one direction to choose, which can be understood in two ways: either as the direction towards the realization of the true self that one intuits is "purposed" for oneself, or as the direction towards God. "This duality of comprehension, however, is no more than a duality of aspects, provided only that I do not apply the name 'God' to a projection of myself or anything of that kind, but to my creator, that is, the author of my uniqueness which cannot be derived from within the world." As Emerson explains, one is to rely on that part of oneself that is cause, and never on oneself as effect, and the two are always to be sharply distinguished. Buber continues: "That a unique human being is created does not mean that it is put into being for a mere existence, but for the fulfillment of a being-intention, an intention of being which is personal, not however in the sense of a free unfolding of infinite singularities, but of a realization of the right in infinite personal shapes. For creation has a goal and the humanly right is service directed in the One direction."[39] And for Emerson the humanly right takes the form of virtue.

Emerson's conception of character fits the characteristics William James cites as typical of the saintly character. First is the feeling of

[38] *The Courage To Be* (New Haven: Yale University Press, 1957), pp. 20–21.
[39] *Good and Evil*, pp. 140–41.

being in a wider, deeper life than that of the temporal order, a deep belief in an ideal power. Next is a sense of the continuation of ideal power in our own life, and a willing submission to it. Third, as a result of submission, is the feeling of immense elation and freedom from confining selfhood. And last, a shifting of the emotional center to spiritual emotions and toward an affirmative rather than negative attitude toward life.[40] "The soul refuses limits, and always affirms an Optimism, never a Pessimism" (*W*, II, 122)—an optimism because, upon the attainment of virtue, the soul sees that virtue is enough.

Finally, character is the superior form because it is the basis of the successful creation of all other forms. Amidst the principle of chaos often exhibited in society and in our own persons, it embodies the principle of order, heaven's first law (*W*, X, 279–80). Rather than reducing religion to ethics or morality, Emerson raises ethics to religious significance; he makes them inseparable aspects of one reality, the whole life. For in character, in the habit of virtue, a man realizes the highest form attainable, a form perfectly expressive of power, the only form that ultimately resolves and fuses being and becoming, God and man, power and form, into an inseparable unity.

[40] *The Varieties of Religious Experience: A Study in Human Nature* (New York: Longmans, Green, 1903), pp. 271–73.

Chapter V

A Golden Impossibility
The Conditions of Emerson's Optimism

WITH THE ATTAINMENT of character the individual resolves man's duality of power and form into a bipolar unity that is in harmony with the Emersonian universe, itself a unity composed of power and form, a unity that is essentially and universally good (*W*, X, 86). This is no more than to say that ultimate reality is one, or God; and that God, Who is all, is good.

To conceive of essential reality as a unity, however, while it makes metaphysical sense, creates problems with regard to the nature of good and evil. Moral dualism—that is, Manicheism—is apparently feasible because it readily explains moral experience. From that experience, one infers that good and evil are two cosmic powers forever in conflict. As a young man, Emerson himself assented to this position: "This is certain—that war is waged in the Universe, without truce or end, between Virtue and Vice; they are Light and Darkness, they cannot harmonize" (*J*, I, 135). The conflict has often been conceived in the simpler terms of spirit and matter, the soul and the body.

But as a philosophy dualism is metaphysically naive—or at least it presents insuperable epistemological problems—and in rejecting it, Emerson faces the problem of accounting for evil on a nondualistic basis. Attempting to do this, he rejects the antagonism of matter and spirit as the origin of evil and declares them to be two aspects of one reality, each a reflection of each, one the phenomenal realization of the laws of the other (*W*, X, 213).

But to say that good and evil are simply two aspects of one reality is unsatisfactory, because it implicitly denies the moral necessity of sharply distinguishing between the two. This is particularly the case when that reality is a unity that is essentially and universally good. In terms of that reality, therefore—in terms of the whole—Emerson has to conceive of evil as negation, the absence of good. "Good is positive. Evil is merely privative, not absolute: it is like cold, which is the privation of heat. All evil is so much death or nonentity. Benevolence is absolute and real" (*W*, I, 124). Defining the metaphysical nature of evil in these terms, it should be noted, does not deny its existence. However one defines the nature of coldness, one implies by the act of defining that there is such a thing as coldness. This conception of evil is, of course, common to many religions—Platonic, Neoplatonic, and Christian—the self-appointed duty of which it has been to demonstrate the unity and goodness of God's order, and to which, therefore, a tragic view of life is false, not because it belies certain facts of existence, but because it incompletely views life from the human perspective alone, and not from the absolute as well.[1] Quite often this conception is native to mysticism. From the mystic's experience of union with the absolute arises his conviction that evil has no separate existence—that God's order is a unity and is essentially good, the goodness containing the evil as a potentiality inseparable from itself.[2] Moses Maimonides, the medieval Jewish theologian, and St. Augustine (who also, at one time, was a Manichean) were notable adherents to this view of evil, and the fact that they were keenly aware of man's sinful nature and of the evil condition of human society indicates that such a view is not incompatible with a stern moral realism. We must bear in mind the influence on this view of the Neoplatonic doctrine of polarity, according to which there is a mystic affinity between the positive and negative poles of reality: in chemistry the positive and negative valences combine, and in algebra the student works with positive and negative signs or quantities and assumes, in Arthur Christy's words, "that the minus quantity is as real as the plus."[3] To say that evil is essentially negative is hardly the same as saying that there is no evil.

Such is the nature of evil considered philosophically in terms of the whole. But we do not ordinarily live in the whole, but in parts, in division; and parts, in the realm of phenomenal existence, have two sides, a good and an evil (*W*, II, 269, 120). Life, therefore, presents to us a moral as well as a philosophical problem, and from these two points of view evil appears entirely different: "Saints are sad, because they behold sin (even when they speculate) from the point of view of the conscience, and not of the intellect; a confusion of thought. Sin, seen from the thought, is a diminution or *less*; seen from the conscience or will, it is pravity or *bad*. The intellect names its shade, absence of light, and no essence. The conscience must feel it as essence, essential evil. This it is not: it has an objective existence, but no subjective" (*W*, III, 79). That is, evil exists as an object only in its relation to the knowing and willing subject, but it has no real or

---

[1] The point is made by Newton Arvin in "The House of Pain," in *Emerson: A Collection of Critical Essays*, ed. Milton R. Konvitz and Stephen E. Whicher (Englewood Cliffs, N.J.: Prentice-Hall, 1962), pp. 54–55.

[2] See William James, *The Varieties of Religious Experience*, pp. 380–81, 388.

[3] *The Orient in American Transcendentalism*, pp. 81–82.

substantial being in its own right. It is not an agent, has no active power. In terms of the absolute, evil is negation; yet in terms of the relative, in human experience, it seems to be positive. We should note Emerson's very careful wording: evil "is" not an essence, yet the conscience "must" feel it as essential, the *must* being a psychological fact and necessity of our moral existence. If, in immediate personal experience, certain impulses and desires did not affect us as bad, we would never be roused to overcome them and develop the discipline of virtue. But these impulses and desires are not evil in themselves; they are evil because we do not subordinate them to, and thus make them expressive of, the universal will, or God. With the attainment of character or virtue itself (which is almost always momentary), the impulses and desires do not seem evil at all, because they are perfectly subordinated to and expressive of the universal will. Therefore: "Self-accusation, remorse, and the didactic morals of self-denial and strife with sin, are in the view we are constrained by our constitution to take of the fact seen from the platform of action"—even though, in terms of the whole, virtue and wickedness are simply the presence or absence, respectively, of God (*W*, I, 204).[4]

With perfect consistency, therefore, Emerson can declare that in the realm of human existence everything has a good and an evil side and then say that beneath that realm, in the essential existence underlying the phenomenal, in the realm of power rather than of form, evil is the absence of essence, being, or God, and in that context can work neither good nor harm (*W*, II, 120–21).[5] With perfect con-

[4] For a good discussion of Emerson's concept of evil, see Mary W. Edrich, "The Rhetoric of Apostasy," *Texas Studies in Language and Literature* 8 (1967): 552–53. Karl Schmid has pointed out how the ideal of personal "wholeness"—the creative integration of the unconscious and the conscious—in much modern depth psychology entails the concept of evil as essential negation: "Aspects of Evil in the Creative," in *Evil*, ed. The Curatorium of The C. G. Jung Institute (Evanston, Ill.: Northwestern University Press, 1967), pp. 231–32.

[5] Matthiessen indicates Melville's reaction to the latter aspect of Emerson's conception: "Against the metaphysical assumptions of 'Spiritual Laws' Melville made his most determined onslaught. When Emerson tried to establish the merely negative nature of evil by stating: 'The good, compared to the evil' which man sees, 'is as his own good to his own evil,' Melville replied: 'A Perfectly Good being therefore would see no evil.—But what did Christ see? He saw what made Him weep. . . . To annihilate all this nonsense read the Sermon on the Mount, and consider what it implies.'" *American Renaissance*, p. 184. Melville did not seem to be aware that one can recognize many evils without believing in evil as essential—that that, in fact, may be all the more cause to weep.

sistency again, Emerson can recognize that the conception of evil as negative does not render our living a simple, easy affirmation: "Human life is made up of the two elements, power and form, and the proportion must be invariably kept if we would have it sweet and sound. Each of these elements in excess makes a mischief as hurtful as its defect. Everything runs to excess; every good quality is noxious if unmixed, and, to carry the danger to the edge of ruin, nature causes each man's peculiarity to superabound" (*W*, III, 65–66). Emerson recognizes the difficulty of attaining virtue, which is another way of saying that he recognizes the force of evil. But, by insisting on viewing evil from an absolute as well as human point of view, he never lets his awareness of its presence all around him overcome his faith in the essential goodness of God's order; the negative aspect of evil, in fact, is a principal element of its essential goodness.

But Emerson does not merely define; he strenuously (almost shrilly) insists that evil is essentially negative: "There is no pure lie, no pure malignity in nature. The entertainment of the proposition of depravity is the last profligacy and profanation. There is no scepticism, no atheism but that. Could it be received into common belief, suicide would unpeople the planet" (*W*, III, 278; see also *W*, IV, 138).[6] By this proposition Emerson is instantly aroused, and we must understand why. He seldom uses philosophical and theological terminology, often attempting to translate it into more poetic and dynamic language, but he advocates nevertheless many old ideas and beliefs. To believe (really believe) in a pure malignity, to adopt a Manichean view, means to him despair, the utter loss of faith in God's power and order. The infinite order no longer believed in, we would have to attempt to substitute an order based on the finite, to live by the senses in the realm of forms alone. The substitution would be foredoomed to failure: "Any distrust of the permanence of laws would paralyze the faculties of man" (*W*, I, 48). Jonathan Edwards makes precisely the same point: "I do suppose there is a great absurdity, in the nature of things simply considered, in supposing that there should be no God, or in denying being in general, and supposing an eternal,

[6] Compare Radoslav Tsanoff's remarks: "That evil *as evil* is rooted and dominant in the very heart of ultimate reality can be the claim only of a pandiabolism, blackest embittered despair. Philosophic pessimism scarcely reaches this extreme: Schopenhauer's Will-to-live is blind and irrational; Hartmann's Unconscious is metalogical; and Mainländer's pre-cosmic Will-to-die is pitiable and pitifully inconsiderate; but not one of them is strictly hateful. The pessimistic poet lets himself go more violently: pity for the woeful creature rouses in him hatred for the Creator of woe." *The Nature of Evil*, p. 7. Not all literary critics have been sufficiently aware of Tsanoff's last point.

absolute, universal nothing."[7] Both assume that either order is absolute or there is none at all—in which case, such absurdity and chaos would produce, in Emerson's view, our total self-destruction.

We have not destroyed ourselves, Emerson believes, because we have acted out of the natural faith, whether acknowledged or even recognized, that the laws of nature are permanent, that a connection, which we call truth, exists between cause and effect, that there is essential order rather than chaos (*W*, IV, 170). Not only is absolute physical order necessary as the basis of moral values, but the belief in such an order is necessary for existence itself. Therefore Emerson considers this belief natural and organic, and considers the very belief itself, apart from its relation to phenomena, to be the significant fact (*W*, III, 74; *W*, VIII, 333). As a product of nature, our most basic beliefs—the beliefs on which we predicate our existence—must in some sense be true; they are not manufactured, they are instinctive, having the same origin as nature, and therefore they must have a truthful relation to nature (*W*, XI, 162–63).

From this foundation Emerson takes the bolder step of affirming that what we find most desirable and indispensable to believe is in fact true (*J*, II, 446–47; see also *W*, I, 59, 63). In a very real sense, Emerson's optimism is a deliberate, pragmatic strategy for living in a hard world. If one believes in fate, he reckons, one might as well believe in a fate for one's good rather than for one's harm (*W*, VI, 24), a proposition reminiscent of Pascal's wager. But Emerson does not pose this solution to the problems of life in order to evade or ignore them: "I cited the instinctive and heroic races as proud believers in Destiny. They conspire with it; a loving resignation is with the event. But the dogma makes a different impression when it is held by the weak and lazy. 'T is weak and vicious people who cast the blame on Fate. The right use of Fate is to bring up our conduct to the loftiness of nature" (*W*, VI, 23–24).[8] Even that aspect of his optimism, based on instinct and on practicality, has a certain harshness to it.

But he bases his optimism on more than instinct and practicality. The fact that there have been men commonly considered to be good serves him as testimony that moral rectitude is possible for us as well (*W*, I, 72–73, 161): "If there ever was a good man, be certain there

[7] *Freedom of the Will*, ed. Paul Ramsay (New Haven, Conn.: Yale University Press, 1957), p. 182.

[8] As Arthur Christy said, "His optimism, instead of being blindness or indifference [to evil], is a most persistent type of therapeutics." *The Orient in American Transcendentalism*, p. 121.

was another and will be more" (*W*, VI, 238). That misdeeds are exploited in the name of goodness indicates that otherwise they could not be so exploited, and that in fact there is such a thing as goodness (*W*, VIII, 316). But finally it is the existence of goodness itself that inspires Emerson's optimistic hope, because its existence indicates a moral sense that is an essential aspect of the total order. "The moral sense is always supported by the permanent interest of the parties. Else, I know not how, in our world, any good would ever get done" (*W*, XI, 125). Emerson's faith rests not so much in men, but in the order of which men are a part, and it is precisely his faith, not his ethical emphasis, that reminds us so much of his Puritan heritage despite the radical differences: " 'T is wonderful where the moral influences come from, since no man is a moralist" (*J*, VIII, 558). "Faith makes us, and not we it, and faith makes its own forms" (*W*, I, 150). Seen in relation to the whole, goodness exists because the whole is a moral order.

Consequently our perspective on life, our "angle of vision," is of the utmost importance (*W*, XII, 10). We must observe phenomena from the perspective of the absolute to see that they are the effects of self-executing laws, to see that these laws are moral, and to see that because of these laws all things, in their relation to the whole, are good and all goes well (*W*, II, 135, 69). From the perception of the laws, or the eternal necessity, and of the essential goodness of that necessity, come a health and a patience by means of which we can understand and therefore cope with the most brutal facts in nature and in human history (*W*, VII, 276).[9] Once again, the perspective of the absolute is not a design for ignoring the harsh facts of life, but a design for coping with them by giving them their proper valuation.

There is no question, however, that Emerson is sometimes inclined to take a view from the absolute at the expense of the human position. Too often he stresses the essential nature of evil without indicating the equally important fact of its effect and function among men. Partly, this stress is a result of Emerson's personal constitution: "I could never give much reality to evil and pain" (*J*, IX, 273).[10] He actually can give a great deal of vivid reality to evil and pain, when he views phenomena from a human perspective, but when he forsakes that perspective his attitude toward human misery—physical and spiritual—can become not softly optimistic, but impatiently heartless.

[9] Santayana thoroughly understood the importance of perspective in Emerson's thought. See *Interpretations of Poetry and Religion* (New York: Scribner's, 1900), p. 221.

[10] Typically, however, Emerson's candor has a saving grace. Consider his terse statement, "I will not affect to suffer" (*J*, III, 298–99).

Pain and suffering, he can say, are merely superficial (see e.g., *W*, VII, 265; *W*, XII, 410).[11]

On the other hand we must realize that Emerson, in insisting that we view life in terms of the absolute, is seeking to show us our proper relation both to the absolute and to society:

> Whilst a man is not grounded in the divine life by his proper roots, he clings by some tendril of affection to society—mayhap to what is best and greatest in it, and in calm times it will not appear that he is adrift and not moored; but let any shock take place in society, any revolution of custom, of law, of opinion, and at once his type of permanence is shaken. The disorder of his neighbors appears to him universal disorder; chaos is come again. But in truth he was already a driving wreck before the wind arose, which only revealed to him his vagabond state. If a man is centred, men and events appear to him a fair image or reflection of that which he knoweth beforehand in himself. If any perversity or profligacy break out in society, he will join with others to avert the mischief, but it will not arouse resentment or fear, because he discerns its impassable limits. He sees already in the ebullition of sin the simultaneous redress. (*W*, XII, 413–14)

Herein may consist the essential difference between Emerson and Hawthorne: both wanted a principle of order by which men could have a meaningful existence, but Emerson felt that that order was to be discovered only in the universal principle of order, the beautiful necessity, not in society, as Hawthorne contended. He doubted the possibility of Emerson's principle, Emerson denied the validity of his: to attain genuine order, men must subordinate the individual ego to the universal ego, the finite order to the infinite order.

When we view nature in perspective, we see that the ordered direction of the whole is ameliorative, beneficial. The ferocity and violence in it are necessary aspects of the evolutionary process, and testify not to anarchy, but to the order that the "indwelling necessity plants . . . on the brow of chaos" (*W*, VI, 35–36, 48). Even in a short-range perspective, there is always a balance, Emerson believes—very

---

[11] F. I. Carpenter considers the main theme of Emerson's thought to be the " 'disparity' between man the suffering, confused, and selfish actor in the human tragedy, which is also 'the divine comedy,' and man the ideal made in the image of God." Because Emerson is mystical, he makes his final evaluation of man's situation from the point of view of God, or the whole, rather than from man, or the part. Hence his view of life is comic rather than tragic, and he can accept—an acceptance difficult for Hawthorne and Melville to understand—the disparity. See *Emerson Handbook* (New York: Hendricks House, 1953), pp. 122–23. Nevertheless, Baritz's assertion that Emerson's optimism is callous and cruel is not without justification. *City on a Hill*, pp. 231–32.

slight, hardly observable, but there nevertheless—favorable to benefit (*W*, I, 372).

This order conducive to benefit is moral. Emerson praises it as perfect, in fact, because it is moral (*W*, II, 101–2). The benefit he speaks of is moral, and he believes that evolution is the process of eliminating evil from this earth, though it will take faith-taxing ages to accomplish (*W*, XI, 238; *W*, X, 191). In the process nature converts all evil to good; the evil exists, but is utilized as a means to good against the evil-doer's own wishes, as Satan is used by God in *Paradise Lost*. But the order that so utilizes evil is moral because the evildoer, though ironically helpful, himself incurs harm (*W*, VII, 289–90). "Whilst a man seeks good ends, he is strong by the whole strength of nature. In so far as he roves from these ends, he bereaves himself of power, of auxiliaries; his being shrinks out of all remote channels, he becomes less and less, a mote, a point, until absolute badness is absolute death" (*W*, I, 124). There is no pure malignity in nature, we should note, but a man can become absolutely bad.

Josiah Royce works out very clearly the implications of Emerson's position. One cannot commit an absolute evil (in Emerson's view, the evil will be converted to good) because that which would be, by itself, an unmixed evil, is an aspect of the organic life of God. "*In him thy evil impulse forms a part of a total good will, as the evil impulse of the good man forms an element in his realization of goodness.*" One can damn oneself, and thus moral justice is done, but one cannot damage the essential goodness of God's order, because that order insures the evil man's just damnation.[12] In the moral process of evolution, in the realm of becoming, all evil acts are converted to good, and in the moral order of God's being, justice is always served. The total order of becoming and being, therefore, is a moral order, and it is good.

Emerson also believes that to view society from the perspective of the whole is to see, analogously to nature, that there is always a slight balance favorable to moral benefit in human history:

the next lesson taught is the continuation of the inflexible law of matter into the subtile kingdom of will and of thought; that if in sidereal ages gravity and projection keep their craft, and the ball never loses its way in its wild path through space,—a secreter gravitation, a secreter projection rule not less tyrannically in human history, and keep the balance of power from age to age unbroken. For though the new element of freedom and an individual has been admitted, yet the primordial atoms are prefigured and predetermined to moral issues, are in search of justice, and ultimate right is done. (*W*, VI, 219)

[12] *The Religious Aspect of Philosophy*, p. 456.

Although the appearance, as he elsewhere says, is immoral, although knaves seem to emerge victorious, although society seems to be handed over from one set of criminals to another, the result is nevertheless moral, and general ends are somehow met (*W*, IV, 185). They are met because the same necessity we see in nature operates in society; the evildoers are assured of their own nothingness, and their deeds, despite the motives, eventually serve the many (*W*, VI, 93–94).

When Emerson views society from a general and historical perspective, he sometimes makes statements that appear to be complacent. But he insists that we have to view it from his perspective in order to realize that society, like nature, is evolving, with the consequence that we must judge particular deeds according to a relative scale. The population, generally speaking, is the best possible at a particular time, and its practices at a particular time are, in terms of the whole, necessary, both for survival and as a means of further progress (*J*, VI, 502; *W*, XI, 151, 160). On the other hand, Emerson very seldom pushes his analogy of nature and society to the extent of believing in inevitable social progress. According to the order of nature, for example, which is superior to the will of men, "there will always be a government of force, where men are selfish" (*W*, III, 220), so that it is up to men to eradicate selfishness if they want a government based on factors other than force. Men are products of nature, but because they are creatures of intelligence and will, their activity has moral value that the laws of nature require to be fulfilled as a condition of amelioration. These laws guarantee an inevitable progression in the realm of lower phenomena, and yet quite consistently guarantee only a conditional progression in human society. Meeting the conditions is part of the essential necessity.

Those conditions are, in probably the simplest terms, to make morality the basis and end of government by enacting the sentiment of love (*W*, XI, 540–41; *W*, I, 252, 254). Without love morality will never be successfully attained, socially speaking, because government reflects the condition of the population. If we read carefully, even Emerson's national optimism is conditional: America, as he sees it, is a land of great hope and expectation, full of "majestic possibilities" of being the greatest civilization in the history of man, if the people fulfill the necessary conditions (*W*, I, 370–71; *W*, XI, 530). Whenever he sounds unduly optimistic, he is convinced that the people will meet the conditions, not that America has a manifest destiny. For even in his most optimistic appraisal of the national situation, "The Fortune of the Republic," he indicates the conditional nature of the country's promise:

this country [is] just passing through a great crisis in its history, as necessary as lactation or dentition or puberty to the human individual. We are in these days settling for ourselves and our descendants questions which, as they shall be determined in one way or the other, will make the peace and prosperity or the calamity of the next ages. The questions of Education, of Society, of Labor, the direction of talent, of character, the nature and habits of the American, may well occupy us, and more the question of Religion. (*W*, XI, 516)

The question to ask ourselves, perhaps, is not whether Emerson's hopes have been realized, but whether his conditions have been met.

And the point is, they must be met by individuals. No matter what kind of formula or theorem he sets up, Emerson always rests at last on the axiom that society is made up of particular men, and that qualitatively the whole is never greater than the sum of its parts, and that, in fact, it has been generally true that some of the parts are greater than the whole, for we should "prefer one Alfred, one Shakespeare, one Milton, one Sidney, one Raleigh, one Wellington, to a million foolish democrats" (*W*, V, 307). Emerson considers it apt that the foolish democrats—that is, the majority of the people in America—are sometimes referred to as the herd or the masses (*W*, I, 106): "But now we are a mob" (*W*, II, 71). The need of course is to reform the masses into men; the reform of an external circumstance, an institution or custom, may correct a particular abuse, but it can never bring about a genuine improvement in society (*W*, I, 281). Men remaining the same, new abuses will rapidly replace the old.

Such thinking violates many canons of modern liberalism. The disparity between the two positions stems apparently from the fact that one position is essentially religious, the other secular. Emerson's concern is almost exclusively qualitative, to the extent that he sometimes slights the importance of quantitative factors. Liberalism—in practice if not in theory—has exhibited an overriding interest in the quantitative aspects of life. It is frankly materialistic. It still has not confronted the basic issue that Emerson raises again and again, and for that reason, perhaps, liberalism is today becoming a byword: we must not confuse quantitative and qualitative values, the circumstances of life and the life itself.

It is Emerson's condition that a fine civilization be achieved "not by the men or materials the statesman uses, but by men transfigured and raised above themselves by the power of principles" (*W*, I, 250). He bases his hope on the belief that such a transfiguration is possible. Men are aware of the great flux and incessant change of all things only because they contain within themselves—by necessity—some principle of stability, of being (*W*, II, 318). Conditions are assuredly bad, but there is in us that which is dissatisfied with those conditions and which aspires to better (*W*, XII, 317).

For this reason the argument which is always forthcoming to silence those who conceive extraordinary hopes of man, namely the appeal to experience, is for ever invalid and vain. We give up the past to the objector, and yet we hope. He must explain this hope. We grant that human life is mean, but how did we find out that it was mean? What is the ground of this uneasiness of ours; of this old discontent? What is the universal sense of want and ignorance, but the fine innuendo by which the soul makes its enormous claim? (*W*, II, 267)

The soul's awareness of evil is probably the essential article of Emerson's optimistic faith.

And this article involves one of his most basic assumptions, namely that every man has a moral sense sufficient for his guidance, provided that he heed it (*J*, III, 389). Emerson once remarked that perhaps "Transcendentalism is the Saturnalia or excess of Faith; the presentiment of a faith proper to man in his integrity" (*W*, I, 338). And when he makes claims that God provides for everyone a moral sentiment that discloses the basic law of His order (*W*, XI, 486), it seems to many that he, too, is suffering from an excess of faith. It is fairly evident, they argue, that there exist men who have no moral sense, and consequently no moral responsibility. Supposing this a hereditary or congenital defect, they ascribe a flaw to the natural order. If it is not congenital, they contend the defect is the result of environmental deprivation, and that the individual is not responsible. Finally, there exists the modern relativist's claim that the so-called moral sense means simply an inculcated awareness of a code of conduct that can be accounted for environmentally: it comes from without, not within, as the abundant variety of contradictory moral codes testifies.

To the first objection, two answers can be made. Frequently the people who are charged with possessing no moral sense simply have a different ethical code—wrong, perhaps, but bespeaking a moral sense just the same. Equally often this objection amounts to a modern variation of innate depravity, and Emerson will not have it. It provides too easy an excuse to shirk and renege responsibility—in his terms, to succumb to the desires of the personal ego and willfully evade the claims of the universal ego—to take the easy out. And his questions remain unanswered: what is the ground of discontent that most of us feel? How do we know that life is mean? And what is the basis of our endless hope? Emerson refuses to let us take refuge from our moral responsibilty. As to the argument of environment, that too can be misused as an easy excuse. For even though environment is a major factor in our lives, at some point, according to Emerson's thinking, men are responsible, even for it. Having failed to enact their moral sentiment, having taken the easy out, men have created conditions of social injustice: the sins of the fathers. . . . A mere change of environment is an insufficient remedy of these conditions, because it does not treat the cause. The eradication of social injustice—not just the eradication of particular abuses—must begin with the moral education of individuals. Otherwise new abuses will simply replace the old. For Emerson, there is no escape from this fact. Further, if environment is responsible for some evil, as most of us feel, it must be responsible for all, including the evil of the powerful, as most of us do not feel, because that would destroy any basis for hope. But we cannot have it, legitimately at least, both ways. Finally, to the relativist's objection it can be said that whatever form it may take, all men innately possess some sense of right and wrong; otherwise they could not ascribe to a mere code of conduct moral significance. The fact that every society has some such code (or codes), however different, and the fact that they can change, simply proves the point. That sense Emerson calls the moral sentiment, and it should not be confused with a particular formulation.[13] Right or wrong, Emerson's claim for the moral sense cannot be easily dismissed.

Most of us in some measure have a moral consciousness—this is simply a basic assumption of any society—and we have a responsibility to it that is not merely passive: "There are no fixtures to men, if we appeal to consciousness. Every man supposes himself not to be fully understood; and if there is any truth in him, if he rests at last on the divine soul, I see not how it can be otherwise. The last chamber, the last closet, he must feel was never opened; there is always a residuum unknown, unanalyzable. That is, every man believes that he has a greater possibility" (*W*, II, 306). This is the other aspect of Emerson's basic assumption about the soul, that its nature provides us the wherewithal (and responsibility) of growth.

Immediately the strenuousness of his optimism becomes apparent, for growth is a responsibility of the individual. It implies that each man is isolated—not entirely, of course, but almost—and therefore "must learn to walk alone" because there is no other way to walk (*W*, X, 119; see also *W*, III, 77, 277). The fact that each man is responsible for himself makes growth difficult, and the conditions in which and by which he must grow are also difficult: "our education is not conducted by toys and luxuries, but by austere and rugged masters,

---

[13] In his excellent discussion of the moral sentiment, Bishop ignores this possibility. See *Emerson on the Soul*, pp. 66–72.

by poverty, solitude, passions, War, Slavery," with the result that "Paradise is under the shadow of swords" (*W*, XI, 236, 240).

The difficulty is accentuated because of the ever-present danger to "craze" ourselves with thinking, to concentrate so exclusively on the problems to be met and all their ambiguous implications that we render ourselves incapable of acting at all "There are objections to every course of life and action," and to indulge them is one aspect of the dangerous excess of power that Emerson warns against (*W*, III, 59). On the other hand, we should think enough to know the limits of our capabilities and the limitations that phenomena set to them (*W*, III, 101). We should as far as necessary adapt our power to the forms of ourselves and the world, achieve a delicate balance of power and form.

The conditions acknowledged, we come to the end Emerson seeks for man. In perhaps his finest essay, "Experience," he says:

To fill the hour,—that is happiness; to fill the hour and leave no crevice for a repentance or an approval. We live amid surfaces, and the true art of life is to skate well on them. Under the oldest mouldiest conventions a man of native force prospers just as well as in the newest world, and that by skill of handling and treatment. He can take hold anywhere. Life itself is a mixture of power and form, and will not bear the least excess of either. To finish the moment, to find the journey's end in every step of the road, to live the greatest number of good hours, is wisdom. (*W*, III, 59–60)[14]

To fill the hour, to balance or fuse power and form, is wisdom, and wisdom is essentially the knowledge and enactment of moral truth. We are to think on living, on doing today the duties of today (*W*, VIII, 328): "Life only avails, not the having lived" (*W*, II, 69). To fill the hour is to "rely on the Law alive and beautiful," which pitilessly uses for its own universal ends the success of our obedience to it and the ruin of our contravention of it (*W*, III, 283). The benefit of obedience is intrinsic, but we should so love the law as to prefer to suffer injustice rather than to do it (*W*, IV, 83–84). Emerson once said that we must choose either power or joy, for we cannot have both (*J*, VI, 282); but the gist of his thought seems to indicate that by humbly submitting to the law, by identifying our personal interests with universal ends (rather than universal ends with our personal interests), we acquire both power and joy.

---

[14] Thoreau, of course, conveyed the same message. Emerson happily quoted from *Walden* Thoreau's statement, "I have never got over my surprise that I should have been born into the most estimable place in all the world, and in the very nick of time too," to which he added, "There's an optimist for you" (*W*, X, 357).

Emerson places his optimistic faith not so much in men as in the ideal, the law, of which men are a part and to which they have access.[15] His insistence that virtue is its own reward, and is a glorious reward of power and joy, is optimistic. But it is strict, for in this doctrine severity and loveliness, law and grace, obedience and joy become one.[16] It is his purpose to attack the very basis of our plight, our evil condition, and thereby stimulate a deep genuine reform (*J*, V, 288–89).[17] Because of the nature of the order in which we live, we have, he believes, the means at hand to resolve the disparity of power and form that makes the human tragedy (*W*, IV, 183). This faith he attempts to arouse in us, to the end of helping to make life "sweet and sound" and living a religious act (*W*, III, 70–71; *W*, VII, 132–33). "A man is a golden impossibilty" (*W*, III, 66). "A man is a god in ruins" (*W*, I, 71). Emerson hopes that we will restore ourselves; that out of our impossible reality we will realize the infinitely possible.

[15] See Fred B. Wahr, *Emerson and Goethe* (Ann Arbor, Mich.: G. Wahr, 1915), pp. 129–30.

[16] See Whicher, *Freedom and Fate*, p. 36, and Edwin D. Mead, "Emerson's Ethics," in *The Genius and Character of Emerson*, ed. Frank B. Sanborn (Boston: J. R. Osgood, 1885), p. 260.

[17] See Henry Miller, "Preface to Three Essays by Henry David Thoreau," in *Thoreau: A Century of Criticism*, ed. Walter Harding (Dallas: Southern Methodist University Press, 1954), p. 164.

Appendix

Emerson's Works

*Page numbers are those of the Centenary Edition.

Index